4-01
(12)
5-00
8in

Other recent books by Joyce Carol Oates

Fiction

RAVEN'S WING

MARYA

SOLSTICE

MYSTERIES OF WINTERTHURN

LAST DAYS

A BLOODSMOOR ROMANCE

ANGEL OF LIGHT

BELLEFLEUR

Nonfiction

THE PROFANE ART: Essays and Reviews

CONTRARIES

NEW HEAVEN, NEW EARTH:
The Visionary Experience in Literature

THE EDGE OF IMPOSSIBILITY:
Tragic Forms in Literature

Joyce Carol Oates

ON BOXING

With photographs by John Ranard

Dolphin/Doubleday · Garden City, New York · 1987

Library of Congress Cataloging-in-Publication Data:
Oates, Joyce Carol, 1938–
    On boxing.
    "Parts of this essay have appeared, in earlier
versions, in the *New York Times* magazine (June 16, 1985)
and the Ontario Review (fall/winter), 1986"—T.p. verso.
    1. Boxing. I. Title.
GV1133.02 1987   796.8'3   86-19710
ISBN 0-385-23890-8
ISBN 0-385-23942-4 (limited edition)

For the contenders . . .

ON BOXING

It's a terrible sport, but it's a sport . . .
the fight for survival is the fight.
—*ROCKY GRAZIANO,*
former middleweight champion of the world

They are young welterweight boxers so evenly matched they might be twins, though one has a red-head's pallor and the other is a dusky-skinned Hispanic. Circling each other in the ring, beneath the glaring lights, trying jabs, tentative left hooks, right crosses that dissolve in mid-air or turn into harmless slaps. How to get inside! How to press an advantage, score a point or two, land a single punch! It seems they have forgotten all they've been trained to do and the Madison Square Garden fight crowd is getting noisy, derisive, impatient. Time is running out. "Those two—what'd they do, wake up this morning and decide they were boxers?" a man behind me says in disgust. (He's dark, nattily dressed, neat-trimmed moustache and tinted glasses. A sophisticated fight fan. Knows all the answers. Two hours later he will be screaming, "Tommy! Tommy! Tommy!" over and over in a paroxysm of grief as, on the giant closed-circuit television screen lowered over the ring, middleweight champion Marvelous Marvin Hagler batters his brash challenger Thomas Hearns into insensibility.)

The young welterweights are surely conscious of the chorus of jeers, boos, and catcalls in this great cavernous space reaching up into the cheap twenty-dollar seats in the balconies amid the constant milling of people in the aisles, the commingled smells of hotdogs, beer, cigarette and cigar smoke, hair oil. But they are locked desperately together in their futile match—circling, "dancing," jabbing, slapping, clinching—now a flurry of light blows, clumsy footwork, yet another sweaty stumbling despairing clinch into the ropes that provokes a fresh wave of derision as the referee helps them apart. Why are they here in the Garden of all places, each fighting, it seems, his first professional fight? Neither wants to hurt the other—neither is angry at the other. When the bell sounds at the end of the fourth and final round the crowd boos a little louder. The Hispanic boy, silky yellow shorts, damp frizzy floating hair, strides about his corner of the ring with his gloved hand aloft—not in defiance of the boos which increase in response to his gesture, or even in acknowledgment of them. It's just something he's doing, something he has seen older boxers do, he's saying *I'm here, I made it, I did it.*

When the decision is announced as a draw the crowd's derision increases in volume. "Get out of the ring!" "Assholes!" "Go home!" Contemptuous male laughter follows the boys up the aisle in their robes, towels about their heads, sweating, breathless. Why had *they* thought they were boxers?

How can you enjoy so brutal a sport, people sometimes ask me.

Or pointedly don't ask.

And it's too complex to answer. In any case I don't "enjoy" boxing in the usual sense of the word, and never have; boxing isn't invariably "brutal"; and I don't think of it as a "sport."

Nor can I think of boxing in writerly terms as a metaphor for something else. No one whose interest began as mine did in childhood—as an offshoot of my father's interest—is likely to think of boxing as a symbol of something beyond itself, as if its uniqueness were merely an abbreviation, or iconographic; though I can entertain the proposition that life is a metaphor for boxing—for one of those bouts that go on and on, round following round, jabs, missed punches, clinches, nothing determined, again the bell and again and you and your opponent so evenly matched it's impossible not to see that your opponent *is* you: and why this struggle on an elevated platform enclosed by ropes as in a pen beneath hot crude pitiless lights in the presence of an impatient crowd?—that sort of hellish-writerly metaphor. Life *is* like boxing in many unsettling respects. But boxing is only like boxing.

For if you have seen five hundred boxing matches you have seen five hundred boxing matches and their common denominator, which certainly exists, is not of primary interest to you. "If the Host is only a symbol," as the Catholic writer Flannery O'Connor once remarked, "I'd say the hell with it."

I am a fighter who walks, talks, and thinks fighting, but I try not to look like it.
—*MARVELOUS MARVIN HAGLER,*
middleweight champion of the world

L ike a dancer, a boxer "is" his body, and is totally identified with it. And the body is identified with a certain weight:

HEAVYWEIGHT—no weight limit
CRUISERWEIGHT—not over 195 pounds
LIGHT HEAVYWEIGHT—not over 175 pounds
MIDDLEWEIGHT—not over 160 pounds
JUNIOR MIDDLEWEIGHT—not over 154 pounds
WELTERWEIGHT—not over 147 pounds
JUNIOR WELTERWEIGHT—not over 140 pounds
LIGHTWEIGHT—not over 135 pounds
JUNIOR LIGHTWEIGHT—not over 130 pounds
FEATHERWEIGHT—not over 126 pounds
JUNIOR FEATHERWEIGHT—not over 122 pounds

BANTAMWEIGHT—not over 118 pounds
FLYWEIGHT—not over 112 pounds

Though the old truism "A good big man will always beat a good little man" has been disproved any number of times (most recently by Michael Spinks in his victory over Larry Holmes) it is usually the case that a boxer invites disaster by fighting out of his weight division: he can "move up" but very likely he can't "bring his punch with him." Where at one time the distinctions between weight were fairly crude (paralleling life's unfairness—the mismatches of most battles outside the ring) boxing promoters and commissions have created a truly Byzantine hierarchy of weights to regulate present-day fights. In theory, the finely calibrated divisions were created to prevent mismatches; in practice, they have the felicitous effect of creating many more "champions" and many more lucrative "title" shots. So it is, an ambitious boxer in our time hopes not only to be a champion but to be a great champion—an immortal; he may try for multiple titles, like Sugar Ray Robinson (world welter- and middleweight champion who tried, and failed, to win the light-heavyweight title from Joey Maxim), Sugar Ray Leonard (world welter- and junior-middleweight champion), Roberto Durán (world light-, welter- and light-middleweight champion who tried, and failed, to move up to middleweight), Alexis Arguello (world featherweight, junior lightweight, and lightweight champion who hoped for a junior welterweight title before his recent retirement).

In order to make his weight the boxer may resort to fasting or vigorous exercise so close to fight time that he risks serious injury: like, most recently, WBA bantamweight champion Richie Sandoval who lost ten pounds in a short period of time and, in his match with Gaby Canizales in March 1986, nearly lost his life as a consequence. When Michael Spinks made boxing history in September 1985 by becoming the first light-heavyweight to win the heavyweight title, as much excited media attention was paid to Spinks's body as to his boxing. For Spinks had accomplished what constituted a *tour de force* of the physical—with the help of his trainer and nutritionist he had created for himself a true heavyweight's body: two hundred pounds of solid muscle. And though his opponent Larry Holmes outweighed him by twenty-odd pounds it scarcely mattered since Spinks had not merely gained weight, he had become a "new" body. And he sustained this remarkable new body for his title defense against Holmes, which he also won. Boxing's fanaticism can go no further.

Why are you a boxer, Irish featherweight champion Barry McGuigan was asked. He said: "I can't be a poet. I can't tell stories . . ."

Each boxing match is a story—a unique and highly condensed drama without words. Even when nothing sensational happens: then the drama is "merely" psychological. Boxers are there to establish an absolute experience, a public accounting of the outermost limits of their beings; they will know, as few of us can know of ourselves, what physical and psychic power they possess—of how much, or how little, they are capable. To enter the ring near-naked and to risk one's life is to make of one's audience voyeurs of a kind: boxing is so intimate. It is to ease out of sanity's consciousness and into another, difficult to name. It is to risk, and sometimes to realize, the agony of which *agon* (Greek, "contest") is the root.

In the boxing ring there are two principal players, overseen by a shadowy third. The ceremonial ringing of the bell is a summoning to full wakefulness for both boxers and spectators. It sets into motion, too, the authority of Time.

The boxers will bring to the fight everything that is themselves, and everything will be exposed—including secrets about themselves they cannot fully realize. The physical self, the maleness, one might say, underlying the "self." There are boxers possessed of such remarkable intuition, such uncanny prescience, one would think they were somehow recalling their fights, not fighting them as we watch. There are boxers who perform skillfully, but mechanically, who cannot improvise in response to another's alteration of strategy; there are boxers performing at the peak of their talent who come to realize, mid-fight, that it will not be enough; there are boxers—including great champions—whose careers end abruptly, and irrevocably, as we watch. There has been at least one boxer possessed of an extraordinary and disquieting awareness not only of his opponent's every move and anticipated move but of the audience's keenest shifts in mood as well, for which he seems to have felt personally responsible— Cassius Clay / Muhammad Ali, of course. "The Sweet Science of Bruising" celebrates the physicality of men even as it dramatizes the limitations, sometimes tragic, more often poignant, of the physical. Though male spectators identify with boxers no boxer behaves like a "normal" man when he is in the ring and no combination of blows is "natural." All is style.

Every talent must unfold itself in fighting. So Nietzsche speaks of the Hellenic past, the history of the "contest"—athletic, and otherwise—by which Greek youths were educated into Greek citizenry. Without the ferocity of competition, without, even, "envy, jealousy, and ambition" in the contest, the Hellenic city, like the Hellenic man, degenerated. If death is a risk, death is also the prize—for the winning athlete.

In the boxing ring, even in our greatly humanized times, death is always a possibility—which is why some of us prefer to watch films or tapes of fights already past, already defined as history. Or, in some instances, art. (Though to prepare for writing this mosaic-like essay I saw tapes of two infamous "death" fights of recent times: the Lupe Pintor–Johnny Owen bantamweight match of 1982, and the Ray Mancini–Duk Koo-Kim lightweight match of the same year. In both instances the boxers died as a consequence of their astonishing resilience and apparent indefatigability—their "heart," as it's known in boxing circles.) Most of the time, however, death in the ring is extremely unlikely; a statistically rare possibility like your possible death tomorrow morning in an automobile accident or in next month's headlined airline disaster or in a freak accident involving a fall on the stairs or in the bathtub, a skull fracture, subarachnoid hemorrhage. Spectators at "death" fights often claim afterward that what happened simply seemed to happen—unpredictably, in a sense accidentally. Only in retrospect does death appear to have been inevitable.

If a boxing match is a story it is an always wayward story, one in which anything can happen. And in a matter of seconds. Split seconds! (Muhammad Ali boasted that he could throw a punch faster than the eye could follow, and he may have been right.) In no other sport can so much take place in so brief a period of time, and so irrevocably.

Because a boxing match is a story without words, this doesn't mean that it has no text or no language, that it is somehow "brute," "primitive," "inarticulate," only that the text is improvised in action; the language a dialogue between the boxers of the most refined sort (one might say, as much neurological as psychological: a dialogue of split-second reflexes) in a joint response to the mysterious will of the audience which is always that the fight be a worthy one so that the crude paraphernalia of the setting —ring, lights, ropes, stained canvas, the staring onlookers themselves—be erased, forgotten. (As in the theater or the church, settings are erased by way, ideally, of transcendent action.) Ringside announcers give to the wordless spectacle a narrative unity, yet boxing as performance is more clearly akin to dance or music than narrative.

To turn from an ordinary preliminary match to a "Fight of the Century" like those between Joe Louis and Billy Conn, Joe Frazier and Muhammad Ali, Marvin Hagler and Thomas Hearns is to turn from listening or half-listening to a guitar being idly plucked to hearing Bach's *Well-Tempered Clavier* perfectly executed, and that too is part of the story's mystery: so much happens so swiftly and with such heart-stopping subtlety you cannot absorb it except to know that something profound is happening and it is happening in a place beyond words.

I try to catch my opponent on the tip of his nose because I try to punch the bone into his brain.
—*MIKE TYSON,*
heavyweight contender

B oxing's claim is that it is superior to life in that it is, ideally, superior to all accident. It contains nothing that is not fully willed.

The boxer meets an opponent who is a dream-distortion of himself in the sense that his weaknesses, his capacity to fail and to be seriously hurt, his intellectual miscalculations—all can be interpreted as strengths belonging to the Other; the parameters of his private being are nothing less than boundless assertions of the Other's self. This is dream, or nightmare: my strengths are not fully my own, but my opponent's weaknesses; my failure is not fully my own, but my opponent's triumph. He is my shadow-self, not my (mere) shadow. The boxing match as "serious, complete, and of a certain magnitude"—to refer to Aristotle's definition of tragedy—is an event that necessarily subsumes both boxers, as any ceremony subsumes its participants. (Which is why one can say, for instance, that the greatest fight of Muhammad Ali's career was one of the few fights Ali lost—the first heroic match with Frazier.)

The old boxing adage—a truism surely untrue—that you cannot be knocked out if you see the blow coming, and if you *will* yourself not to be knocked out, has its subtler, more daunting significance: nothing that happens to the boxer in the ring, including death—"his" death—is not of his own will or failure of will. The suggestion is of a world-model in which we are humanly responsible not only for our own acts but for those performed against us.

Which is why, though springing from life, boxing is not a metaphor for life but a unique, closed, self-referential world, obliquely akin to those severe religions in which the individual is both "free" and "determined"— in one sense possessed of a will tantamount to God's, in another totally helpless. The Puritan sensibility would have understood a mouth filling with blood, an eye popped out of its socket—fit punishment for an instant's negligence.

A boxing trainer's most difficult task is said to be to persuade a young boxer to get up and continue fighting after he has been knocked down. And if the boxer has been knocked down by a blow he hadn't seen coming— which is usually the case—how can he hope to protect himself from being knocked down again? and again? The invisible blow is after all—invisible.

"Normal" behavior in the ring would be unbearable to watch, deeply shameful: for "normal" beings share with all living creatures the instinct to persevere, as Spi-

noza said, in their own being. The boxer must somehow learn, by what effort of will non-boxers surely cannot guess, to inhibit his own instinct for survival; he must learn to exert his "will" over his merely human and animal impulses, not only to flee pain but to flee the unknown. In psychic terms this sounds like magic. Levitation. Sanity turned inside out, "madness" revealed as a higher and more pragmatic form of sanity.

The fighters in the ring are time-bound—surely nothing is so excruciatingly long as a fiercely contested three-minute round—but the fight itself is timeless. In a sense it becomes all fights, as the boxers are all boxers. By way of films, tapes, and photographs it quickly becomes history for us, even, at times, art. Time, like the possibility of death, is the invisible adversary of which the boxers—and the referee, the seconds, the spectators—are keenly aware. When a boxer is "knocked out" it does not mean, as it's commonly thought, that he has been knocked unconscious, or even incapacitated; it means rather more poetically that he has been knocked out of Time. (The referee's dramatic count of ten constitutes a metaphysical parenthesis of a kind through which the fallen boxer must penetrate if he hopes to continue in Time.) There are in a sense two dimensions of Time abruptly operant: while the standing boxer is *in time* the fallen boxer is *out of time.* Counted out, he is counted "dead"—in symbolic mimicry of the sport's ancient tradition in which he would very likely be dead. (Though, as we may recall, the canny Romans reserved for themselves as spectators the death blow itself: the triumphant gladiator was obliged to wait for a directive from outside the arena before he finished off his opponent.)

If boxing is a sport it is the most tragic of all sports because more than any human activity it consumes the very excellence it displays—its drama is this very consumption. To expend oneself in fighting the greatest fight of one's life is to begin by necessity the downward turn that next time may be a plunge, an abrupt fall into the abyss. *I am the greatest* says Muhammad Ali. *I am the greatest* says Marvelous Marvin Hagler. You always think you're going to win, Jack Dempsey wryly observed in his old age, otherwise you couldn't fight at all. The punishment—to the body, the brain, the spirit—a man must endure to become even a moderately good boxer is inconceivable to most of us whose idea of personal risk is largely ego-related or emotional. But the punishment as it begins to show in even a young and vigorous boxer is closely gauged by his rivals, who are waiting for him to slip. (After junior-welterweight champion Aaron Pryor won a lackluster fight last year a younger boxer in his weight division, interviewed at ringside, said with a smile: "My mouth is watering." And there was twenty-nine-year-old Billy Costello's bold statement—"If I can't beat an old man [of thirty-three] then I should retire"—shortly before his bout with Alexis Arguello, in which he was knocked out in an early round.)

In the ring, boxers inhabit a curious sort of "slow" time—amateurs never box beyond three rounds, and for most amateurs those nine minutes are exhausting—while outside the ring they inhabit an alarmingly accelerated time. A twenty-three-year-old boxer is no longer young in the sense in which a twenty-three-year-old man is young; a thirty-five-year-old is frankly old. (Which is why Muhammad Ali made a tragic mistake in continuing his career after he had lost his title for the second time—to come out of retirement, aged thirty-eight, to fight Larry Holmes; and why Holmes made a similar mistake, years later, in needlessly exposing himself to injury, as well as professional embarrassment, by meeting with the light-heavyweight champion Michael Spinks. The victory of the thirty-seven-year-old Jersey Joe Walcott over the thirty-year-old Ezzard Charles, for the heavyweight title in 1951, is *sui generis.* And Archie Moore is *sui generis.*) All athletes age rapidly but none so rapidly and so visibly as the boxer.

So it is, the experience of watching great fighters of the past is radically different from having seen them perform when they were reigning champions. Jack Johnson, Jack Dempsey, Joe Louis, Sugar Ray Robinson, Rocky Marciano, Muhammad Ali, Joe Frazier—as spectators we know not only how a fight but how a career ends. The trajectory not merely of ten or fifteen rounds but that of an entire life . . .

> *Everything that man esteems*
> *Endures a moment or a day.*
> *Love's pleasure drives his love away,*

The painter's brush consumes his dreams;
The herald's cry, the soldier's tread
Exhaust his glory and his might:
Whatever flames upon the night
Man's own resinous heart has fed.

—WILLIAM BUTLER YEATS, *from "The Resurrection"*

When I see blood, I become a bull.
—MARVIN HAGLER

I have no difficulty justifying boxing as a sport because I have never thought of it as a sport.

There is nothing fundamentally playful about it; nothing that seems to belong to daylight, to pleasure. At its moments of greatest intensity it seems to contain so complete and so powerful an image of life—life's beauty, vulnerability, despair, incalculable and often self-destructive courage—that boxing *is* life, and hardly a mere game. During a superior boxing match (Ali-Frazier I, for instance) we are deeply moved by the body's communion with itself by way of another's intransigent flesh. The body's dialogue with its shadow-self—or Death. Baseball, football, basketball—these quintessentially American pastimes are recognizably sports because they involve play: they are games. One *plays* football, one doesn't *play* boxing.

Observing team sports, teams of adult men, one sees how men are children in the most felicitous sense of the word. But boxing in its elemental ferocity cannot be assimilated into childhood. (Though very young men box, even professionally, and many world champions began boxing in their early or mid-teens. By the time he was sixteen Jack Dempsey, rootless and adrift in the West, was fighting for small sums of money in unrefereed saloon fights in which—in the natural course of things—he might have been killed.) Spectators at public games derive much of their pleasure from reliving the communal emotions of childhood but spectators at boxing matches relive the murderous infancy of the race. Hence the occasional savagery of boxing crowds—the crowd, largely Hispanic, that cheered as the Welshman Johnny Owen was pounded into insensibility by the Mexican bantamweight champion Lupe Pintor, for instance—and the excitement when a man begins to seriously bleed.

Marvelous Marvin Hagler, speaking of blood, is speaking, of course, of his own.

Considered in the abstract the boxing ring is an altar of sorts, one of those legendary spaces where the laws of a nation are suspended: inside the ropes, during an officially regulated three-minute round, a man may be killed at his opponent's hands but he cannot be legally murdered. Box-

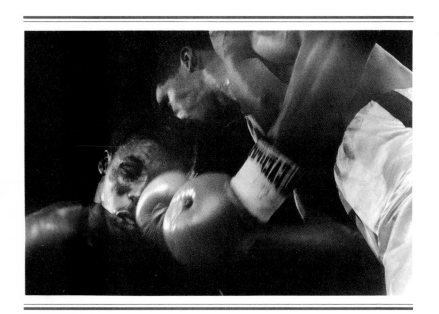

ing inhabits a sacred space predating civilization; or, to use D. H. Lawrence's phrase, before God was love. If it suggests a savage ceremony or a rite of atonement it also suggests the futility of such gestures. For what possible atonement is the fight waged if it must shortly be waged again . . . and again? The boxing match is the very image, the more terrifying for being so stylized, of mankind's collective aggression; its ongoing historical madness.

I hate to say it, but it's true—
I only like it better when pain comes.
—FRANK "THE ANIMAL" FLETCHER,
former middleweight contender

Years ago in the early 1950s when my father first took me to a Golden Gloves boxing tournament in Buffalo, New York, I asked him why the boys wanted to fight one another, why they were willing to get hurt. As if it were an explanation my father said, "Boxers don't feel pain quite the way we do."

Pain, in the proper context, is something other than pain.

Consider: Gene Tunney's single defeat in a thirteen-year career of great distinction was to a notorious fighter named Harry Greb who seems to have been, judging from boxing lore, the dirtiest fighter in history. Greb was infamous for his fouls—low blows, butting, "holding and hitting," rubbing his laces against an opponent's eyes, routine thumbing—as well as for a frenzied boxing style in which blows were thrown from all directions. (Hence, "The Human Windmill.") Greb, who died young, was a world middleweight champion for three years but a flamboyant presence in boxing circles for a long time. After the first of his several fights with Greb the twenty-two-year-old Tunney was so badly hurt he had to spend a week in bed; he'd lost an astonishing two quarts of blood during the fifteen-round fight. Yet, as Tunney said some years later:

> Greb gave me a terrible whipping. He broke my nose, maybe with a butt. He cut my eyes and ears, perhaps with his laces . . . My jaw was swollen from the right temple down the cheek, along under the chin and partway up the other side. The referee, the ring itself, was full of blood . . . But it was in that first fight, in which I lost my American light-heavyweight title, that I knew I had found a way to beat Harry eventually. I was fortunate, really. If boxing in those days had been afflicted with the Commission doctors we have today—

*who are always poking their noses into the ring and
examining superficial wounds—the first fight with Greb
would have been stopped before I learned how to beat
him. It's possible, even probable, that if this had happened I would never have been heard of again.*

Tunney's career, in other words, was built upon pain.
Without it he would never have moved up into Dempsey's
class.

Tommy Loughran, light-heavyweight champion in
the years 1927–29, was a master boxer greatly admired
by other boxers. He approached boxing literally as a science—as Tunney did—studying his opponents' styles and
mapping out ring strategy for each fight, as boxers and
their trainers commonly do today. Loughran rigged up
mirrors in his basement so that he could watch himself as
he worked out, for, as he said, no boxer ever sees himself
quite as he appears to his opponent. He sees the opponent
but not himself as an opponent. The secret of Loughran's
career was that his right hand broke easily so that he was
forced to use it only once each fight: for the knockout
punch or nothing. "I'd get one shot then the agony of the
thing would hurt me if the guy got up," Loughran said.
"Anybody I ever hit with a left hook I knocked flat on his
face, but I would never take a chance for fear if my [left
hand] goes, I'm done for."

Both Tunney and Loughran, it is instructive to note,
retired from boxing well before they were forced to retire.
Tunney became a highly successful businessman, and

Loughran a highly successful sugar broker on the Wall Street commodities market. (Just to suggest that boxers are not invariably stupid, illiterate, or punch-drunk.)

Then there was Carmen Basilio!—much loved for his audacious ring style, his hit-and-be-hit approach. Basilio was world middle- and welterweight champion 1953–57, stoic, determined, a slugger willing to get hit in order to deal powerful counter-punches of his own. Onlookers marveled at the punishment Basilio seemed to absorb though Basilio insisted that he didn't get hit the way people believed. And when he was hit, and hit hard—

> *People don't realize how you're affected by a knockout punch when you're hit on the chin. It's nerves is all it is. There's no real concussion as far as the brain is concerned. I got hit on the point of the chin [in a match with Tony DeMarco in 1955]. It was a left hook that hit the right point of my chin. What happens is it pulls your jawbone out of your socket from the right side and jams it into the left side and the nerve there paralyzed the whole left side of my body, especially my legs. My left knee buckled and I almost went down, but when I got back to my corner the bottom of my foot felt like it had needles about six inches high and I just kept stamping my foot on the floor, trying to bring it back. And by the time the bell rang it was all right.*

Basilio belongs to the rough-and-tumble era of LaMotta, Graziano, Zale, Pep, Saddler; Gene Fullmer, Dick Tiger, Kid Gavilan. An era when, if two boxers wanted to fight dirty, the referee was likely to give them license, or at least not to interfere.

Of Muhammad Ali in his prime Norman Mailer observed, "He worked apparently on the premise that there was something obscene about being hit." But in fights in his later career, as with George Foreman in Zaire, even Muhammad Ali was willing to be hit, and to be hurt, in order to wear down an opponent. Brawling fighters—those with "heart" like Jake LaMotta, Rocky Graziano, Ray Mancini—have little choice but to absorb terrible punishment in exchange for some advantage (which does not in any case always come). And surely it is true that some boxers (see Jake LaMotta's autobiographical *Raging Bull)* invite injury as a means of assuaging guilt, in a Dostoyevskian exchange of physical well-being for peace of mind. Boxing is about being hit rather more than it is about hitting, just as it is about feeling pain, if not devastating psychological paralysis, more than it is about winning. One sees clearly from the "tragic" careers of any number of boxers that the boxer prefers physical pain in the ring to the absence of pain that is ideally the condition of ordinary life. If one cannot hit, one can yet be hit, and know that one is still alive.

It might be said that boxing is primarily about maintaining a body capable of entering combat against other well-conditioned bodies. Not the public spectacle, the fight itself, but the rigorous training period leading up to it demands the most discipline, and is believed to be the chief cause of the boxer's physical and mental infirmities. (As a boxer ages his sparring partners get younger, the game itself gets more desperate.)

The artist senses some kinship, however oblique and one-sided, with the professional boxer in this matter of training. This fanatic subordination of the self in terms of a wished-for destiny. One might compare the time-bound public spectacle of the boxing match (which could be as brief as an ignominious forty-five seconds—the record for a title fight!) with the publication of a writer's book. That which is "public" is but the final stage in a protracted, arduous, grueling, and frequently despairing period of preparation. Indeed, one of the reasons for the habitual attraction of serious writers to boxing (from Swift, Pope, Johnson to Hazlitt, Lord Byron, Hemingway, and our own Norman Mailer, George Plimpton, Ted Hoagland, Wilfrid Sheed, Daniel Halpern, et al.) is the sport's systematic cultivation of pain in the interests of a project, a life-goal: the willed transposing of the sensation we know as pain (physical, psychological, emotional) into its polar opposite. If this is masochism—and I doubt that it is, or that it is simply—it is also intelligence, cunning, strategy. It is an act of consummate self-determination—the constant re-establishment of the parameters of one's being. To not only accept but to actively invite what most sane creatures avoid—pain, humiliation, loss, chaos—is to experience the present moment as already, in a sense, past. *Here* and *now* are but part of the design of *there* and *then:* pain now

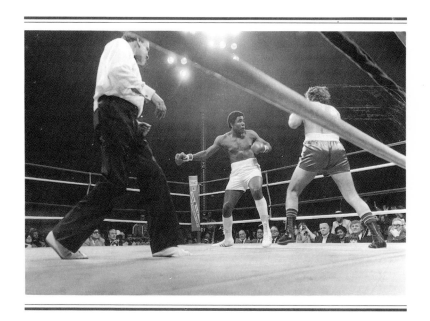

but control, and therefore triumph, later. And pain itself is miraculously transposed by dint of its context. Indeed, it might be said that "context" is all.

The novelist George Garrett, an amateur boxer of some decades ago, reminisces about his training period:

> *I learned something . . . about the brotherhood of boxers. People went into this brutal and often self-destructive activity for a rich variety of motivations, most of them bitterly antisocial and verging on the psychotic. Most of the fighters I knew of were wounded people who felt a deep, powerful urge to wound others at real risk to themselves. In the beginning. What happened was that in almost every case, there was so much self-discipline required and craft involved, so much else besides one's original motivations to concentrate on, that these motivations became at least cloudy and vague and were often forgotten, lost completely. Many good and experienced fighters (as has often been noted) become gentle and kind people . . . They have the habit of leaving all their fight in the ring. And even there, in the ring, it is dangerous to invoke too much anger. It can be a stimulant, but is very expensive of energy. It is impractical to get mad most of the time.*

Of all boxers it seems to have been Rocky Marciano (still our only undefeated heavyweight champion) who trained with the most monastic devotion; his training methods have become legendary. In contrast to reckless fighters like Harry "The Human Windmill" Greb, who kept in condition by boxing all the time, Marciano was willing to seclude himself from the world, including his wife and family, for as long as three months before a fight. Apart from the grueling physical ordeal of this period and the obsessive preoccupation with diet and weight and muscle tone, Marciano concentrated on one thing: the upcoming fight. Every minute of his life was defined in terms of the opening second of the fight. In his training camp the opponent's name was never mentioned in Marciano's hearing, nor was boxing as a subject discussed. In the final month Marciano would not write a letter since a letter related to the outside world. During the last ten days before a fight he would see no mail, take no telephone calls, meet no new acquaintances. During the week before the fight he would not shake hands. Or go for a ride in a car, however brief. No new foods! No dreaming of the morning after the fight! For all that was not *the fight* had to be excluded from consciousness. When Marciano worked out with a punching bag he saw his opponent before him, when he jogged he saw his opponent close beside him, no doubt when he slept he "saw" his opponent constantly— as the cloistered monk or nun chooses by an act of fanatical will to "see" only God.

Madness?—or merely discipline?—this absolute subordination of the self. In any case, for Marciano, it worked.

Tommy Hearns was a little cocky,
and I had something for him.
—MARVIN HAGLER

No sport is more physical, more direct, than boxing. No sport appears more powerfully homoerotic: the confrontation in the ring—the disrobing—the sweaty heated combat that is part dance, courtship, coupling—the frequent urgent pursuit by one boxer of the other in the fight's natural and violent movement toward the "knockout": surely boxing derives much of its appeal from this mimicry of a species of erotic love in which one man overcomes the other in an exhibition of superior strength and will. The heralded celibacy of the fighter-in-training is very much a part of boxing lore: instead of focusing his energies and fantasies upon a woman the boxer focuses them upon an opponent. Where Woman has been, Opponent must be.

As Ali's Bundini Brown has said: "You got to get the hard-on, and then you got to keep it. You want to be careful not to lose the hard-on, and cautious not to come."

Most fights, however fought, end with an embrace

between the boxers after the final bell—a gesture of mutual respect and apparent affection that appears to the onlooker to be more than perfunctory. Rocky Graziano sometimes kissed his opponents out of gratitude for the fight. One might wonder if the boxing match leads irresistibly to this moment: the public embrace of two men who otherwise, in public or in private, could never approach each other with such passion. Though many men are loudly contemptuous of weakness (as if eager to dissociate themselves from it: as during a boxing match when one or both boxers are unwilling to fight) a woman is struck by the admiration, amounting at times to awe, they will express for a man who has exhibited superior courage while losing his fight. And they will express tenderness for injured boxers, even if it is only by way of commentary on photographs: the picture of Ray Mancini after his second defeat by Livingstone Bramble, for instance, when Mancini's face was hideously battered (photographs in *Sports Illustrated* and elsewhere were gory, near-pornographic); the much-reprinted photograph of the defeated Thomas Hearns being carried to his corner in the arms of an enormous black man (a bodyguard, one assumes) in solemn formal attire—Hearns the "Hit Man" now helpless, semiconscious, looking very like a black Christ taken from the cross. These are powerful, haunting, unsettling images, cruelly beautiful, inextricably bound up with boxing's primordial appeal.

Yet to suggest that men might love and respect one another directly, without the violent ritual of combat, is to misread man's greatest passion—for war, not peace. Love, if there is to be love, comes second.

I know I'm not a bad fighter. I try so hard at some-thing I like doing. I love boxing. I dream of being a fighter. I see myself winning the title. I don't know which one. I see myself being picked up, carried around, getting my belt. Sometimes I see it in slow motion . . .
—a thirty-four-year-old welterweight
who has lost nearly all his fights,
usually by knockouts

A n "opponent" is known in the boxing trade as a man who loses, and is dependable. Matched with a younger, promising boxer with financial backing he will give a decent showing, he will very likely not collapse in the opening seconds of the opening round, and he will not, certainly, mar the record of the other boxer. He may have dreams of winning a "title" but his value to the trade is that he helps to build up (i.e., to inflate) another boxer's record. His name is always unknown—indeed, he is likely to have several names or aliases. His career is a foregone conclusion: he has none. He works for a living by way of being a human punching bag.

Opponents are also known as "stiffs" and "bums"— as in Joe Louis's "Bum-of-the-Month" matches after Louis had cleared the heavyweight division of serious contenders for his title.

• The world's consistently highest-paid athletes are American boxers—but it does not follow that boxers as a class are the highest paid athletes. The very opposite is the case. Impoverished people prostitute themselves in ways available to them, and boxing on its lowest levels offers an opportunity for men to make a living of a kind. In fact, if a boxer is fortunate and isn't injured, boxing will pay him better wages than most of the jobs available to unskilled and uneducated men in our post-industrial society. (After Michael Spinks won an Olympic gold medal he quit boxing and went to work scrubbing floors and cleaning toilets in a St. Louis chemical factory. But conditions in the factory were so bad he had to return, he said, to boxing: "Heck, breathing those chemicals, I could have died faster there than in the ring.") And boxing in circumstances where casino gambling and not safety is a priority—Atlantic City, for instance, and not New York City with its stringent boxing regulations—is likely to be highly tempting. The top of the pyramid is small, the base broad, shading out into the anonymous subsoil of humanity.

The Ring magazine, "The Bible of Boxing," publishes the results of over one thousand fights in every issue. Even boxing's many ranked and overrated boxers constitute a small number of the men who are licensed to box in the United States and elsewhere. *The Ring Record Book* lists such boxers as Johnny D. (who has lost sixteen fights in a row, twelve by knockouts); Marcus D. (who won only his first fight years ago and has lost each subsequent match); Obie G. (who has had nine fights and has been knocked out nine times); Irving B. (who has had seven fights and has been knocked out seven times, always in the first or second round). It is such professional opponents who account for the unblemished records of others —for clearly, the up-and-coming with their straight wins and zero losses cannot have been fighting one another.

• (During the 1920s when boxing was officially banned in New York, boxers fought in private clubs, not unlike speakeasies, in wholly unsupervised circumstances. Budd Schulberg writes that during the years boxing was outlawed there were in fact many more matches in New York City than there are now: each borough had its own clubs, matches were held every night of the week, boxers of all weights, ages, experience, and abilities were thrown haphazardly together, and, if a match resulted in death, the boxer's body was likely to be dumped without identification in the river.) •

With the complicity of managers and promoters, boxers of this class frequently fight under several aliases, and even with present-day regulations (in New York and Pennsylvania, for instance, a fighter who has been knocked out is automatically suspended for ninety days; in New Jersey, for sixty days) it is extremely difficult to prevent them from doing themselves harm. Desperation for money or simply for "fame" cannot be regulated. Identification is made not with boxing's limitless supply of losers but with boxing's very few stars, as in any other profession in which the individual can be, by way of his own intransigent will, glorified. As a trainer of opponents says, perhaps not even cynically: "There's a new guy walking in the gym every day."

When you're fighting you're fighting
for one thing: money.
—JACK DEMPSEY,
former heavyweight champion of the world

That boxing is our most controversial sport, always, it seems, on the very threshold of oblivion, has not prevented it from having become a multimillion-dollar business.

For the past several years the three highest-paid athletes in the world have been American boxers. (In 1985 Larry Holmes reported an income of a little more than

$6.5 million; Marvin Hagler, a little more than $5 million; Thomas Hearns, approximately $5 million. By contrast, the fourth highest-paid athlete, a celebrated football player, reported an income of only—only!—$3 million.) In his long and spotty career Jack Dempsey earned $3,500,000—prodigious for his time, though the equivalent today of only $28 million. Muhammad Ali, who earned somewhere beyond $70 million through his long career, is generally believed to be the most highly paid athlete in world history; his successor Larry Holmes is believed to have earned nearly that much. (Though figures vary, and Holmes's career, at the time of this writing, is still extant; he claims to have $99 million in the bank— with more to come.) Individual boxing matches sometimes bring in extraordinary sums for boxers, even accounting for the money drawn off by promoters: the losing challenger Thomas Hearns made at least $7 million in his eight-minute fight with Marvin Hagler, while Hagler made at least $7.5 million; for the first of his highly publicized matches with Roberto Durán in 1980—which he lost on points—the popular welterweight champion Sugar Ray Leonard was paid $10 million (to Durán's $2 million). One of the focal arguments for a title fight between Marvin Hagler and Sugar Ray Leonard was that the gate would very likely be the highest in all of boxing history: a promoter's dream. And none of these figures takes into account various subsidiary earnings from television appearances and commercials which, in Leonard's case, have certainly been substantial.

Indeed, these subsidiary earnings have become, for many boxers, the measure of their worth beyond the ring: the assessment, in dollars, of "consumer acceptance" of their images. *(The Ring* magazine is beginning to note the sums earned by boxers giving television endorsements of products . . . a new kind of ring "record," it might be said.)

Money has drawn any number of retired boxers back into the ring, frequently with tragic results. The most notorious example still remains Joe Louis, who, in a desperate attempt to pay money owed in back taxes, continued fighting well beyond the point at which he could defend himself against younger heavyweights. After a career of seventeen years during which Louis virtually came to typify boxing internationally he was finally—and ignominiously—stopped by the much younger Rocky Marciano (who was as grieved by his victory as Louis by the defeat). Louis then took on a degrading second career as a professional wrestler, which ended abruptly in 1956 when, aged forty-two, he suffered injuries to his heart muscles after three-hundred-pound "Rocky Lee" stepped on his chest.

Ezzard Charles, Jersey Joe Walcott, Joe Frazier, Muhammad Ali, most recently Larry Holmes—each heavyweight champion or ex-champion continued fighting well beyond the point at which he could safely defend himself. If Ali had retired permanently at the age of thirty-six—if he had not, contrary to his physician's advice, insisted upon fighting, two years later, the much-younger Larry Holmes—perhaps his story would have a happier ending. (When Ali was told in the mid-1970s to retire by his personal physician Ferdie Pacheco his response was to fire Pacheco.) Of all heavyweight champions only Rocky Marciano, to whom fame and money were evidently not of paramount importance, was wise enough to retire before he was defeated.

In any case, a boxer's passion for money—for the prodigious sums earned by a very few champions—does not account for the fact that a public is willing, if not eager, to pay them these sums. Private and public obsessions mimic one another but are not identical.

*Boxing is the sport to which
all other sports aspire.
—GEORGE FOREMAN,*
former heavyweight champion of the world

At least in theory and by way of tradition boxing is a sport. But what *is* sport?—and why is a man, *in* sport, not the man he is or is expected to be at other times?

Consider the history of gladiatorial combat as the Romans practiced it, or caused it to be practiced, from approximately 265 B.C. to its abolishment by Theodoric in A.D. 500. In the ancient world, among part-civilized nations, it was customary after a battle to sacrifice prisoners of war in honor of commanders who had been killed. It also became customary to sacrifice slaves at the funerals of all persons of importance. But then—for what reason?— for amusement, or for the sake of "sport"?—the condemned slaves were given arms and urged to defend themselves by killing the men who were ordered to kill them. Out of this evolution of brute sacrifice into something approaching a recognizable sporting contest the notorious phenomenon of Roman gladitorial combat—death as mass amusement—gradually arose. Surely there is nothing quite like it in world history.

At first the contests were performed at the funeral pyre or near the sepulcher, but, with the passage of time, as interest in the fighting detached itself from its ostensibly religious context, matches were moved to the Forum, then to the Circus and amphitheaters. Contractors emerged to train the slaves, men of rank and political importance began to keep "families" of gladiators, upcoming fights were promoted and advertised as sporting contests are today, shows lasting as long as three days increased in number and popularity. Not the mere sacrifice of helpless individuals but the "sport" of the contest excited spectators, for, though the instinct to fight and to kill is surely qualified by one's personal courage, the instinct to watch others fight and kill is evidently inborn. When the boxing fan shouts, "Kill him! Kill him!" he is betraying no peculiar individual pathology or quirk but asserting his common humanity and his kinship, however distant, with the thousands upon thousands of spectators who crowded into the Roman amphitheaters to see gladiators fight to the death. That such contests for mass amusement endured not for a few years or even decades but for centuries should arrest our attention.

According to Petronius the gladiators took the following oath: "We swear, after the dictation of Eumolpus, to suffer death by fire, bonds, stripes, and the sword; and whatever else Eumolpus may command, as true gladiators we bind ourselves body and mind to our master's service." Their courage became legendary. Cicero referred to it as a model for all Roman citizens—that one should be willing to suffer nobly in the defense of the Commonwealth. In general, gladiators were slaves and condemned criminals who could hope to prolong their lives or even, if they were champions, to gain freedom; but impoverished freemen often fought as well. With the passage of time, paralleling and surely contributing to what we see as the decadence of Rome, even men of rank volunteered to compete publicly. (Under Nero, that most notorious of Roman emperors, such wild exhibitions flourished. It is estimated that during his reign from A.D. 54 to 68 as many as one thousand aristocrats performed as gladiators in one way or another, in fights fair, handicapped, or fixed. At times even women of rank competed—which matches were no doubt particularly noteworthy.) So drawn to these violent sports were Roman aristocrats that the Emperor Augustus was finally moved to issue an edict forbidding them to train as gladiators.

The origins of gladiatorial boxing are specifically Greek. According to tradition a ruler named Thesus (circa 900 B.C.) was entertained by the spectacle of two matched fighters, seated, facing each other, hammering each other to death with their fists. Eventually the men fought on their feet and covered their fists with leather thongs; then with leather thongs covered with sharp metal spikes—the cestus. A ring of some kind, probably a circle, became a neutral space to which an injured boxer might temporarily retreat. When the Romans cultivated the sport it became extremely popular: one legendary cestus-champion was said to have killed 1,425 opponents. Winning gladiators were widely celebrated as "kings of athletes" and heroes for all. By confirming in the public arena the bloody mortality of other men they established for themselves, as champions always do, a kind of immortality.

So it happens that the wealthier and more advanced a society, the more fanatic its interest in certain kinds of sport. Civilization's trajectory is to curve back upon itself —naturally? helplessly?—like the mythical snake biting its own tail and to take up with passion the outward signs and gestures of "savagery." While it is plausible that emotionally effete men and women may require ever more extreme experiences to arouse them, it is perhaps the case too that the desire is not merely to *mimic* but, magically, to *be* brute, primitive, instinctive, and therefore innocent. One might then be a person for whom the contest is not mere self-destructive play but life itself; and the world, not in spectacular and irrevocable decline, but new, fresh, vital, terrifying and exhilarating by turns, a place of wonders. It is the lost ancestral self that is sought, however futilely. Like those dream-remnants of childhood that year by year continue to elude us but are never abandoned, still less despised, for that reason.

Roman gladiatorial combat was abolished under the Christian emperors Constantine and Theodoric, and its practice discontinued forever. Boxing as we know it in the United States derives solely from English bare-knuckle prizefighting of the eighteenth century and from an entirely different conception of sport.

The first recorded account of a bare-knuckle fight in England—between "a gentleman's footman and a butcher"—is dated 1681 and appeared in a publication called the *London Protestant Mercury*. This species of fight, in which maiming and death were not the point, was known as a "Prize Fight" or the "Prize Ring," and was public entertainment of an itinerant nature, frequently attached to village fairs. The Prize Ring was a movable space created by spectators who formed a loose circle by holding a length of rope; the Prize Fight was a voluntary contest between two men, usually a "champion" and a "challenger," unrefereed but governed by rudimentary rules of fair play. The challenge to fight was put to a

crowd by a fighter and his accomplices and if any man wanted to accept he tossed his hat into the ring—hence the political expression with its overtone of bellicosity— and the fight was on. Bets were commonly placed on which man would knock the other down first or draw "first blood." Foul play was actively discouraged by the crowd; the fighters shook hands after the fight. "The No- ble Art," as prizefighting was called, began as a low-life species of entertainment but was in time enthusiastically supported by sporting members of the aristocracy and the upper classes.

England's earliest bare-knuckle champion was a man named James Figg who won the honor in 1719. The last of the bare-knuckle champions was the American heavy- weight John L. Sullivan whose career—from approxi- mately 1882 to 1892—overlapped both bare-knuckle fighting and gloved boxing as established under the rules of the Marquis of Queensberry which are observed, with some elaboration, to the present time. The most signifi- cant changes were two: the introduction of leather gloves (mainly to protect the hand, not the face—a man's knuck- les are easily broken) and the third man in the ring, the referee, whose privilege it is to stop the fight at his own discretion, if he thinks a boxer has no chance of winning or cannot defend himself against his opponent. With the introduction of the referee the crudeness of "The Noble Art" passes over into the relative sophistication of boxing.

The "third man in the ring," usually anonymous so far as the crowd is concerned, appears to many observers no more than an observer himself, even an intruder; a ghostly presence as fluid in motion and quick-footed as the boxers themselves (indeed, he is frequently an ex-boxer). But so central to the drama of boxing is the referee that the spectacle of two men fighting each other unsupervised in an elevated ring would seem hellish, if not obscene—life rather than art. The referee makes boxing possible.

The referee is our intermediary in the fight. He is our moral conscience extracted from us as spectators so that, for the duration of the fight, "conscience" need not be a factor in our experience; nor need it be a factor in the boxers' behavior. (Asked if boxers are ever sorry for having hurt their opponents, Carmen Basilio replied: "Sorry? Are you kidding? Boxers are never sorry.") Which is not to say that boxers are always and forever without conscience: all boxers are different, and behave differently at different times. But there are occasions when a boxer who is trapped in the ropes and unable to fall to the canvas while being struck repeatedly is in danger of being killed unless the referee intervenes—the attacking boxer has been trained not to stop his attack while his opponent is still technically standing. In the rapidly escalating intensity of the fight only the referee remains neutral and objective.

Though the referee's role is highly demanding and it has been estimated that there are perhaps no more than a

dozen really skilled referees in the world, it seems necessary in the drama of the fight that the referee himself
possesses no dramatic identity: referees' names are rarely
remembered after a fight except by seasoned boxing fans.
Yet, paradoxically, the referee's participation is crucial.
He cannot control what happens in the ring but he can
control to a degree *that* it happens—he is responsible for
the fight if not for the individual fighters' performances.
In a match in which boxing skills and not merely fighting
are predominant the referee's role can be merely func-
tional, but in a fiercely contested match it is of incalculable importance. The referee holds the power of life and
death at certain times since his decision to terminate a
fight, or to allow it to continue, can determine a boxer's
fate. (One should know that a well-aimed punch with a
heavyweight's full weight behind it can have the equivalent force of ten thousand pounds—a blow that must be
absorbed by the brain in its jelly sac.) In the infamous
Benny Paret–Emile Griffith fight of March 1962 the referee Ruby Goldstein was said to have stood paralyzed as
Griffith trapped Paret in the ropes, striking him as many
as eighteen times in the head. (Paret died ten days later.)
Boxers are trained not to quit. If knocked down, they try
to get up to continue the fight, even if they can hardly
defend themselves. The primary rule of the ring—to defend oneself at all times—is both a parody and a distillation of life.

In the past—well into the 1950s—it was not customary for a referee to interfere with a fight, however brutal

and one-sided. A boxer who kept struggling to his feet after having been knocked down, or, like the intransigent Jake LaMotta in his sixth and final fight with Sugar Ray Robinson in 1951, refused to fall to the canvas though he could no longer defend himself and had become a human punching bag, was simply left to his fate. The will of the crowd—and overwhelmingly it *is* the will of the crowd—that one man defeat the other totally and irrevocably, was honored. Hence the bloody "great" fights of boxing's history—Dempsey's triumph over Willard, for instance—inconceivable today.

It should be understood that "boxing" and "fighting," though always combined in the greatest of boxers, can be entirely different and even unrelated activities. Amateur boxers are trained to win their matches on points; professionals usually try for knockouts. (Not that professionals are more violent than amateurs but why trust judges?—and the knockout is dramatically spectacular.) If boxing is frequently, in the lighter weights especially, a highly complex and refined skill, belonging solely to civilization, fighting belongs to something predating civilization, the instinct not merely to defend oneself—for how has the masculine ego ever been assuaged by so minimal a response to threat?—but to attack another and to force him into absolute submission. This accounts for the electrifying effect upon a typical fight crowd when fighting suddenly emerges out of boxing—when, for instance, a boxer's face begins to bleed and the fight seems to enter a new and more dangerous phase. The flash of red is the visible sign of the fight's authenticity in the eyes of many spectators and boxers are justified in being proud, as many are, of their facial scars.

If the "violence" of boxing seems at times to flow from the crowd, to be a heightened expression of the crowd's delirium—rarely transmitted by television, by the way—the many restraints and subtleties of boxing are possible because of the "third man in the ring," a counter of sorts to the inchoate wash of emotion beyond the ropes and the ring apron: our conscience, as I've indicated, extracted from us, and granted an absolute authority.

. . . Whether [this] makes me a humanist or a voyeur, I'm not sure.
—JOHN SCHULIAN,
sportswriter

Writers have long been attracted to boxing, from the early days of the English Prize Ring to the present time. Its most immediate appeal is that of the spectacle, in itself wordless, lacking a language, that requires others to define it, celebrate it, complete it. Like all extreme but perishable human actions boxing excites not

only the writer's imagination, but also his instinct to bear witness. Before film and tape, this instinct must have been particularly acute. (Consider a sport that often took place illegally, many of its most famous fights fought on barges, on islands, in outlaw territory between states, involving the risk of arrest for both performers and observers: what passion!) And boxers have frequently displayed themselves, inside the ring and out, as characters in the literary sense of the word. *Extravagant fictions without a structure to contain them.*

In the days of the Prize Ring, accounts of fights were often in verse, accompanied by cartoon-like drawings, printed on broadsides, and sold by itinerant salesmen. From approximately 1700 onward—according to boxing historian Pierce Egan—most English newspapers, including the fashionable *The Times,* carried detailed accounts of fights; and in 1818 Egan brought out the first edition of his famous *Boxiana: Sketches of Ancient and Modern Pugilism,* which covered the Prize Ring from its earliest days to Egan's own when, though wildly popular, Prize Fighting was officially illegal and announcements of impending matches were by way of rumor. (Any number of editions of *Boxiana* have been printed, the most recent being in the 1970s.) Egan's zest for his outlaw subject is communicated in prose of a particularly vigorous kind—colorful, direct, blunt, "masculine," yet as subtly and as wittily nuanced as that of his eighteenth-century predecessors Defoe, Swift, Pope, Fielding, Churchill. It is Egan who called fighting "the Sweet Science of Bruising" and it is

Egan whom A. J. Liebling most frequently cites and acknowledges as his master in *The Sweet Science,* a *boxiana* of modern times much admired by boxing enthusiasts.

(I sense myself uneasily alone in disliking much of Liebling, for his relentlessly jokey, condescending, and occasionally racist attitude toward his subject. Perhaps because it was originally published in *The New Yorker* in the early 1950s *The Sweet Science: Boxing and Boxiana—a Ringside View* is a peculiarly self-conscious assemblage of pieces, arch, broad in its humor, rather like situation comedy in which boxers are "characters" depicted for our amusement. Liebling is uncertain even about such champions as Louis, Marciano, and Robinson—should one revere, or mock? And he is pitiless when writing about "Hurricane" Jackson, a black boxer cruelly called an animal, an "it," because of his poor boxing skills and what Liebling considers his mental inferiority. The problem for Liebling and for *The New Yorker* must have been how to sell a blood sport like boxing to a genteel, affluent readership to whom the idea of men fighting for their lives would have been deeply offensive; how to suggest boxing's drama while skirting boxing's tragedy. It is a problem that, for all his verbal cleverness, Liebling never entirely solves.)

A good deal has been made of Ernest Hemingway's attraction to boxing yet Hemingway never wrote about boxing with the sympathy or perception with which he wrote about bullfighting; "Fifty Grand" and "The Battler" are not among Hemingway's best short stories, and his portrait of the "Princeton middleweight" Robert Cohn in *The Sun Also Rises* is a startlingly crude piece of Jew-baiting, in which Cohn's boxing skills are irrelevant. (When, provoked beyond endurance, Cohn knocks down Jake Barnes and his drunken friend, the scene passes by so swiftly it makes virtually no impression on the reader.)

Far more canny and knowledgeable is Norman Mailer, whose essays on Cassius Clay/Muhammad Ali and his coevals, and on the "aesthetics of the arena" generally, are as good as anything ever written on the subject. Mailer's strength lies in his recognition that the boxers are *other*—though he does not say so, even in the long extravagant meditation of *The Fight* (its title in homage to Hazlitt's great essay), it seems clear to this reader at least that Mailer cannot establish a connection between himself and the boxers: he tries heroically but he cannot understand them and so he is forever excluded from what, unthinkingly, they represent: an ideal (because unthinking, unforced) masculinity, beyond all question. It is this recognition of his exclusion—an exclusion very nearly as complete as, say, the exclusion of a woman from boxing's codified world—that allows for the force of Mailer's vision. And since the great champions of our time have been black, Mailer's preoccupation with masculinity is a preoccupation with blackness as well. Hence these characteristic flights of metaphysical fancy that strike the ear with the poignancy of a lovesick lament:

If [the heavyweights] become champions they begin to have inner lives like Hemingway or Dostoyevsky, Tolstoy or Faulkner, Joyce or Melville or Conrad or Lawrence or Proust . . . Dempsey was alone and Tunney could never explain himself and Sharkey could never believe himself nor Schmeling nor Braddock, and Carnera was sad and Baer an indecipherable clown; great heavyweights like Louis had the loneliness of the ages in their silence, and men like Marciano were mystified by a power which seemed to have been granted them. With the advent, however, of the great modern Black heavyweights, Patterson, Liston, then Clay and Frazier, perhaps the loneliness gave way to what it had been protecting itself against—a surrealistic situation unstable beyond belief. Being a Black heavyweight champion in the second half of the twentieth century (with Black revolutions opening all over the world) was now not unlike being Jack Johnson, Malcolm X and Frank Costello all in one . . .

(EXISTENTIAL ERRANDS, *"King of the Hill"*)

It cannot be a coincidence that everyone's favorite boxing novel, Leonard Gardner's *Fat City*, is a novel less about boxing than about the strategies of self-deception; a handbook of sorts in failure, in which boxing functions as the natural activity of men totally unequipped to comprehend life. The boxers of Gardner's Stockton, California—that notorious fight town—seem to exist in a world claustrophobic as a training gym, with no more awareness of the great boxers of their time (would not Cassius Clay himself have been their contemporary?) than of politics and "society" in general. *Fat City* is the underside of the American dream, in which men with some minimal skill in a dangerous sport are hired to fight one another for pitifully small purses: it is a measure of the novel's irony that victory, for such stakes, is hardly to be distinguished from failure. Leonard Gardner seems to have written no other fiction, but his several articles on boxing—published in such magazines as *Sports Illustrated* and *Esquire*—display a remarkable gift for realizing, as if from the inside, the psychology of the man born to fight, the man who knows nothing *but* fighting, no matter the suicidal nature of his calling.

W. C. Heinz and Ted Hoagland have written highly regarded novels about boxing, *The Professional* and *The Circle Home* respectively, though Hoagland's novel is something of an anomaly: there are no fights in it, only training scenes, rendered with a mesmerizing kinetic precision. Budd Schulberg, Irwin Shaw, Nelson Algren, Ring Lardner, James Farrell, John O'Hara, Jack London—all have written stories about boxers, of varying worth and seriousness.

What might be called the romance of boxing—and even the sordid, filmed, *is* romance—underlies a number of Hollywood movies of similarly uneven worth, the most extraordinary being Martin Scorsese's award-winning *Raging Bull,* in which Robert De Niro almost literally transforms himself into Jake LaMotta. Other notable films

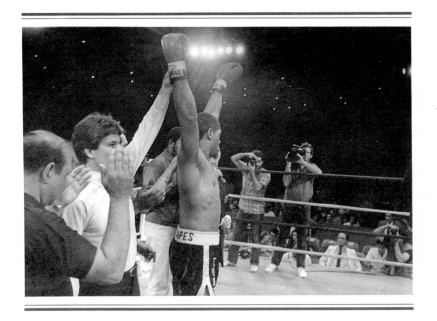

in this genre are *Fat City, Champion, Somebody Up There Likes Me* (based on the Rocky Graziano autobiography), *The Harder They Fall, The Set-Up, The Champ, Body and Soul, Requiem for a Heavyweight,* and *The Great White Hope*—the last two based on successful plays. And then there are the "Rocky" movies, scarcely about boxing as we know it (Rocky and his heavyweight opponents are, for one thing, ludicrously encumbered with bodybuilders' physiques, not boxers') but effective as pop-iconographic success stories starring Sylvester Stallone as Rocky, "The Italian Stallion," the sweet tough guy, the perpetual underdog who cannot lose even against overwhelming odds. Rocky is a comic book boxer, his matches are comic book matches, like the exploits of his look-alike Rambo, who embodies even more powerfully than Rocky America's fascination with the (male) *isolato* whose orientation to the world is purely physical. Yet it is significant, certainly, that Stallone made Rocky a boxer, in homage to heavyweight champion Rocky Marciano, whose ring style he imitates—to a degree.

Boxing has often stimulated first-rate sportswriting, that most taxing of genres. Among contemporary sportswriters John Schulian (of the Philadelphia *Daily News)* and Hugh McIlvanney (of the English *The Observer)* are outstanding for the consistently high quality of their prose and for what might be called their rigorously analytical approach to their subject: not merely *what,* and *how,* but in fact *why*—why does boxing exist, why are men (and some women) fascinated by it, what does it tell us about the human predicament? Schulian's *Writers' Fighters* and McIlvanney's *McIlvanney on Boxing* bring together columns published over a period of time but are notable for the unity of their respective visions. Neither writer takes his subject for granted, nor does he draw back from examining the ambivalent relationship between the man who writes about boxing and boxing itself, "the sweet science of bruising." Other sports draw forth other responses, but boxing is, here as elsewhere, a special case. In no other sport is the connection between performer and observer so intimate, so frequently painful, so unresolved.

That no other sport can elicit such *theoretical* anxiety lies at the heart of boxing's fascination for the writer. It is the thing in itself but it is also its meaning to the individual, shifting and problematic as a blurred image in a mirror. The writer contemplates his opposite in the boxer, who is all public display, all risk and, ideally, improvisation: he will know his limit in a way that the writer, like all artists, never quite knows his limit—for we who write live in a kaleidoscopic world of ever-shifting assessments and judgments, unable to determine whether it is revelation or supreme self-delusion that fuels our most crucial efforts. Setting aside for a moment the problem of incompetent or biased judges, of the kind that gave Michael Spinks a victory over Larry Holmes in Spinks's title defense of April 1986, or had Ray Mancini outpointing Livingstone Bramble in the first of their two matches, the boxer's world is not an ambiguous one: he quickly comes to know his worth in a context of other boxers. Indeed, it is impossible not to know it. "Promising" careers are ended in a matter of seconds; "comebacks" are revealed as mere mistakes; a young and unranked contender (like "Lightning" Lonnie Smith in his title match against junior welterweight champion Billy Costello) leaps immediately to the top. There can be no ambiguity about Marvin Hagler's defeat of John Mugabi, or Thomas Hearns's defeat of James Shuler, or the unexpected loss of his bantamweight title by Richie Sandoval to Gaby Canizales— the near loss, it seemed to some observers, of Sandoval's very life. This sense of an ending, a limit, a final and incontestable judgment—boxing in its greatest moments suggests the bloody fifth acts of classic tragedies, in which that mysterious element we call "plot" achieves closure.

For some writers the fascination has to do, as I've suggested earlier, with boxing's dazzlingly explicit display of masochism—"masochism" in its loosest, most suggestive, one might say poetic sense. For, contrary to stereotyped notions, boxing is primarily about being, and not giving, hurt. (Which the most distinguished boxing movies—*Raging Bull, Fat City, Champion*—suggest most graphically.) To move through pain to triumph—or the semblance of triumph—is the writer's, as it is the boxer's, hope. The moment of visceral horror in a typical fight, at least as I experience it, is that moment when one boxer loses control, cannot maintain his defense, begins to waver, falter, fall back, rock with his opponent's punches which he can no longer absorb; the moment in which the fight is turned around, and which an entire career, an entire life, may end. It is not an isolated moment but *the* moment—mystical, universal. The defeat of one man is the triumph of the other: but we are apt to read this "triumph" as merely temporary and provisional. Only the defeat is permanent.

When I used to dream about boxing, or about abstract, inconclusive matches between dream-opponents whose faces I could not see, I thought of boxing as a knot of sorts, tightly, cruelly knotted, there to be untied. You can't, but you must, untie it. You must—but you can't. If you untie one knot you will be confronted with another and beyond that another, and another: rounds, matches, career, "life." The difference for the boxer is that loss, humiliation, shame are only part of the risk—physical injury, even death, awaits as well. One is punished for one's failure as Kafka imagined one might be punished for one's sins, the sentence etched into flesh, killing even as it pronounces judgment.

. . . Down there in the stable a hollow square of faces in the lantern light, the white faces on three sides, the black faces on the fourth, and in the center two of [Sutpen's] wild negroes fighting, naked, fighting not as white men fight, with rules and weapons, but as negroes fight to hurt one another quick and bad.

—from WILLIAM FAULKNER'S ABSALOM, ABSALOM!

Some time ago one of the southern states adopted a new method of capital punishment. Poison gas supplanted the gallows. In its earliest stages, a microphone was placed inside the sealed death chamber so that scientific observers might hear the words of the dying prisoner . . . The first victim was a young Negro. As the pellet dropped into the container, and gas curled upward, through the microphone came these words: "Save me, Joe Louis. Save me, Joe Louis. Save me, Joe Louis . . ."
—MARTIN LUTHER KING, JR.,
quoted in Chris Mead,
CHAMPION—JOE LOUIS,
BLACK MAN IN WHITE AMERICA

It's hard being black. You ever been black?
I was black once—when I was poor.
—LARRY HOLMES,
former WBC heavyweight champion

One's first impression is that professional boxers fighting together appear to be angry with each other, since their actions mimic anger, even rage. Why else hit, and try to injure, another person? Naturally this initial impression is misleading—boxing is "work" to most boxers and emotion has little part in it, or should have little. Indeed, highly successful champions from Jack Dempsey to Larry Holmes have insisted they fought only for money. To acknowledge other motives would suggest *machismo's* vulnerability.

Yet in a deeper sense boxers *are* angry, as even a superficial knowledge of their lives indicates. And boxing is fundamentally about anger. It is in fact the only sport in which anger is accommodated, ennobled. It is the only human activity in which rage can be transposed without equivocation into art.

Some observers—among them men—believe that boxers are angry because they are men; and anger, for men, is a means of asserting dominance over other men— a tool, one might say, of the manly trade. Yet it is reasonable to assume that boxers fight one another because the legitimate objects of their anger are not accessible to them. There is no political system in which the spectacle of two men fighting each other is not a striking, if unintended, image of the political impotence of most men (and women): You fight what's nearest, what's available, what's ready to fight you. And, if you can, you do it for money.

If boxers as a class are angry one would have to be willfully naïve not to know why. For the most part they constitute the disenfranchised of our affluent society, they are the sons of impoverished ghetto neighborhoods in which anger, if not fury, is appropriate—rather more, perhaps, than Christian meekness and self-abnegation. (It

was only in prison that Sonny Liston, one of twenty-five children born to a sharecropper's family in rural Arkansas, had enough to eat.) Where there is peace, Nietzsche theorizes, the warlike man attacks himself, but what precisely is "peace"? and where, in ghetto neighborhoods of unspeakable squalor and malaise, is it to be located? Boxing may be a way of cruelly assaulting one's self but it is most immediately a way of transcending one's fate. Going to war, like Marvin Hagler, and making millions of dollars from it, is distinctly American.

The history of boxing—of fighting—in America is very much one with the history of the black man in America. It hardly needs to be said that the armed services of recent times are comprised, for the most part, of black youths; the majority of soldiers who fought, and died, in Vietnam were black. Perhaps it is less well known that in the American South, before the Civil War, white slave owners commonly pitted their Negro slaves against one another in combat, and made bets on the results. To prevent the slaves' escape, or, perhaps, to make poetically graphic the circumstances of the black men's degradation, iron collars resembling dog collars were fixed about their necks and attached to chains. Often the fights were to the death. The onlookers, of course, were white; and male.

"Fighting slave collars," as they are called, are sometimes exhibited as artifacts of a specifically American/Southern history; sometimes as instruments of torture.

At the present time, when most outstanding boxers

are black, Hispanic, or Mexican, purely "Caucasian" men begin to look anemic in the ring; a white-skinned champion (the enormously popular Barry McGuigan, for instance) is something of an anomaly, and white-skinned contenders (Gerry Cooney, Matthew Hilton, Gene Hatcher, et al.) very much in demand. One of the most popular athletes in Canada is the young welterweight Shawn O'Sullivan, so alarmingly *white* a figure in the ring, in the first fight of his televised for an American audience, the viewer sensed almost at once that his more experienced black opponent, Simon Brown, would handily defeat him. The anxieties of an earlier era—that black men would prove more "manly" than white men if allowed to fight them in fair, public fights—would seem to have come true.

It is perhaps not commonly known that a Negro heavyweight championship title existed from 1902 to 1932 when many white champions (including John L. Sullivan, Jim Jeffries, Jack Dempsey) refused to fight blacks. (In 1925 Dempsey pointedly refused to meet Harry Wills —"The Black Menace"—in a title fight urged upon him by many observers.) One wonders: who were the true world's champions in those years? And of what value are historical records when they record so blatantly the prejudices of a dominant race? As recently as 1982, after decades of exemplary black boxers—from Jack Johnson to Joe Louis to Sugar Ray Robinson to Muhammad Ali— heavyweight champion Larry Holmes drew racist slurs

and insults when he defended his title against the over-rated and overpromoted White Hope challenger Gerry Cooney (whose prefight picture, and not Holmes's, ran on the cover of *Time* magazine). It is said that on the day of the match in Las Vegas President Reagan's Secret Service installed a special telephone hookup in Cooney's dressing room so that the white boxer could be immediately congratulated if he won; there was no matching telephone in the black champion's dressing room.

Much has been made of Holmes's legendary bitterness, as if having earned millions of dollars—and millions of dollars for others—should tidily erase the humiliations of the past. Surely this is a psychological impossibility? Lashing out against the memory of Rocky Marciano after the first of his two controversial losses to Michael Spinks, Holmes may well have been lashing out against all white champions: "—to be technical: Rocky Marciano couldn't carry my jockstrap."

Men and women with no personal or class reason for feeling anger are inclined to dismiss the emotion, if not piously condemn it, in others. Why such discontent? why such unrest? why so *strident?* Yet this world is conceived in anger—and in hatred, and in hunger—no less than it is conceived in love: that is one of the things that boxing is about. It is so simple a thing it might be overlooked.

Those whose aggression is masked, or oblique, or unsuccessful, will always condemn it in others. They are

likely to think of boxing as "primitive"—as if inhabiting
the flesh were not a primitive proposition, radically inap-
propriate to a civilization supported by and always subordinate to physical strength: missiles, nuclear warheads.
The terrible silence dramatized in the boxing ring is the
silence of nature before man, before language, when the
physical being alone was God.

In any case, anger is an appropriate response to certain intransigent facts of life, not a motiveless malignancy
as in classic tragedy but a fully motivated and socially
coherent impulse. Impotence takes many forms—one of
them being the reckless physical expenditure of physical
potency.

What time is it?—"Macho Time"!
—Hector "Macho Man" Camacho,
WBC lightweight champion

I don't want to knock my opponent out.
I want to hit him, step away, and watch him hurt.
I want his heart.
—Joe Frazier,
former heavyweight champion of the world

A fairy-tale proposition: the heavyweight champion is the most dangerous man on earth: the most feared, the most manly. His proper mate is very likely the fairy-tale princess whom the mirrors declare the fairest woman on earth.

Boxing is a purely masculine activity and it inhabits a purely masculine world. Which is not to suggest that most men are defined by it: clearly, most men are not. And though there are female boxers—a fact that seems to surprise, alarm, amuse—women's role in the sport has always been extremely marginal. (At the time of this writing the most famous American woman boxer is the black

champion Lady Tyger Trimiar with her shaved head and theatrical tiger-striped attire.) At boxing matches women's role is limited to that of card girl and occasional National Anthem singer: stereotypical functions usually performed in stereotypically zestful feminine ways—for women have no natural place in the spectacle otherwise. The card girls in their bathing suits and spike heels, glamour girls of the 1950s, complement the boxers in their trunks and gym shoes but are not to be taken seriously: their public exhibition of themselves involves no risk and is purely decorative. Boxing is for men, and is about men, and *is* men. A celebration of the lost religion of masculinity all the more trenchant for its being lost.

In this world, strength of a certain kind—matched of course with intelligence and tirelessly developed skills— determines masculinity. Just as a boxer is his body, a man's masculinity is his use of his body. But it is also his triumph over another's use of his body. The Opponent is always male, the Opponent is the rival for one's own masculinity, most fully and combatively realized. Sugar Ray Leonard speaks of coming out of retirement to fight one man, Marvin Hagler: "I want Hagler. I need that man." Thomas Hearns, decisively beaten by Hagler, speaks of having been obsessed with him: "I want the rematch badly . . . there hasn't been a minute or an hour in any day that I haven't thought about it." Hence women's characteristic repugnance for boxing per se coupled with an intense interest in and curiosity about men's fascination with it. Men fighting men to determine worth (i.e., mascu-

linity) excludes women as completely as the female experience of childbirth excludes men. And is there, perhaps,
some connection?

In any case, raw aggression is thought to be the peculiar province of men, as nurturing is the peculiar province
of women. (The female boxer violates this stereotype and
cannot be taken seriously—she is parody, she is cartoon,
she is monstrous. Had she an ideology, she is likely to be
a feminist.) The psychologist Erik Erikson discovered
that, while little girls playing with blocks generally create
pleasant interior spaces and attractive entrances, little
boys are inclined to pile up the blocks as high as they can
and then watch them fall down: "the contemplation of
ruins," Erikson observes, "is a masculine specialty." No
matter the mesmerizing grace and beauty of a great boxing match, it is the catastrophic finale for which everyone
waits, and hopes: the blocks piled as high as they can
possibly be piled, then brought spectacularly down.
Women, watching a boxing match, are likely to identify
with the losing, or hurt, boxer; men are likely to identify
with the winning boxer. There is a point at which male
spectators are able to identify with the fight itself as, it
might be said, a Platonic experience abstracted from its
particulars; if they have favored one boxer over the other,
and that boxer is losing, they can shift their loyalty to the
winner—or, rather, "loyalty" shifts, apart from conscious
volition. In that way the ritual of fighting is always honored. The high worth of combat is always affirmed.

Boxing's very vocabulary suggests a patriarchal

world taken over by adolescents. This world is young. Its focus is youth. Its focus is of course *macho—machismo* raised beyond parody. To enter the claustrophobic world of professional boxing even as a spectator is to enter what appears to be a distillation of the masculine world, empty now of women, its fantasies, hopes, and stratagems magnified as in a distorting mirror, or a dream.

Here, we find ourselves through the looking-glass. Values are reversed, evaginated: a boxer is valued not for his humanity but for being a "killer," a "mauler," a "hitman," an "animal," for being "savage," "merciless," "devastating," "ferocious," "vicious," "murderous." Opponents are not merely defeated as in a game but are "decked," "stiffed," "starched," "iced," "destroyed," "annihilated." Even the veteran sportswriters of so respectable a publication as *The Ring* are likely to be pitiless toward a boxer who has been beaten. Much of the appeal of Roberto Durán for intellectual boxing *aficionados* no less than for those whom one might suppose his natural constituency was that he seemed truly to want to kill his opponents: in his prime he was the "baby-faced assassin" with the "dead eyes" and "deadpan" expression who once said, having knocked out an opponent named Ray Lampkin, that he hadn't trained for the fight—next time he would kill the man. (According to legend Durán once felled a horse with a single blow.) Sonny Liston was another champion lauded for his menace, so different in spirit from Floyd Patterson as to seem to belong to another subspecies; to watch Liston overcome Patterson in tapes of their fights in the early 1960s is to watch the defeat of "civilization" by something so elemental and primitive it cannot be named. Masculinity in these terms is strictly hierarchical—two men cannot occupy the same space at the same time.

At the present time twenty-year-old Mike Tyson, Cus D'Amato's much-vaunted protégé, is being groomed as the most dangerous man in the heavyweight division. He is spoken of with awe as a "young bull"; his strength is prodigious, at least as demonstrated against fairly hapless, stationary opponents; he enters the arena robeless—"I feel more like a warrior"—and gleaming with sweat. He does not even wear socks. His boxing model is not Muhammad Ali, the most brilliant heavyweight of modern times, but Rocky Marciano, graceless, heavy-footed, indomitable, the man with the massive right-hand punch who was willing to absorb five blows in the hope of landing one. It was after having broken Jesse Ferguson's nose in a recent match that Tyson told reporters that it was his strategy to try to drive the bone back into the brain . . .

The names of boxers! *Machismo* as sheer poetry.

Though we had, in another era, "Gentleman Jim" Corbett (world heavyweight champion, 1892–97); and the first black heavyweight champion, Jack Johnson (1908–15) called himself "Li'l Arthur" as a way of commenting playfully on his powerful physique and savage ring style. (Johnson was a white man's nightmare: the black man who mocked his white opponents as he humiliated them with his fists.) In more recent times we had "Sugar Ray" Robinson and his younger namesake "Sugar Ray" Leonard. And Tyrone Crawley, a thinking man's boxer, calls himself "The Butterfly." But for the most part a boxer's ring name is chosen to suggest something more ferocious: Jack Dempsey of Manassa, Colorado, was "The Manassa Mauler"; the formidable Harry Greb was "The Human Windmill"; Joe Louis was, of course, "The Brown Bomber"; Rocky Marciano, "The Brockton Blockbuster"; Jake LaMotta, "The Bronx Bull"; Tommy Jackson, "Hurricane" Jackson; Roberto Durán, "Hands of Stone" and "The Little Killer" variously. More recent are Ray "Boom-Boom" Mancini, Thomas "Hit-Man" Hearns, James "Hard Rock" Green, Al "Earthquake" Carter, Frank "The Animal" Fletcher, Donald "The Cobra" Curry, Aaron "The Hawk" Pryor, "Terrible" Tim Witherspoon, "Bonecrusher" Smith, Johnny "Bump City" Bumphus, Lonnie "Lightning" Smith, Barry "The Clones Cyclone" McGuigan, Gene "Mad Dog" Hatcher, Livingstone "Pit Bull" Bramble, Hector "Macho Man" Camacho. "Marvelous" Marvin Hagler changed his name legally to Marvelous Marvin Hagler before his fight with Thomas Hearns brought him to national prominence.

It was once said by José Torres that the *machismo* of boxing is a condition of poverty. But it is not, surely, a condition uniquely of poverty? Or even of adolescence? I think of it as the obverse of the feminine, the denial of the feminine-in-man that has its ambiguous attractions for all men, however "civilized." It is a remnant of another, earlier era when the physical being was primary and the warrior's masculinity its highest expression.

We fighters understand lies. What's a feint?
What's a left hook off the jab?
What's an opening? What's thinking one thing
and doing another . . . ?
—JOSÉ TORRES,
former light-heavyweight champion of the world

One of the primary things boxing is about is lying. It's about systematically cultivating a double personality: the self in society, the self in the ring. As the chess grandmaster channels his powerful aggressive impulses onto the game board, which is the world writ small, so the "born" boxer channels his strength into the ring, against the Opponent. And in the ring, if he is a good boxer and not a mere journeyman, he will cultivate yet another split personality, to thwart the Opponent's game plan vis-à-vis *him*. Boxers, like chess players, must think on their feet—must be able to improvise in mid-fight, so to speak.

(And surely it is championship chess, and not box-ing, that is our most dangerous game—at least so far as psychological risk is concerned. Megalomania and psycho-sis frequently await the grand master when his extraordi-nary mental powers can no longer be discharged onto the chessboard.)

After his upset victory against WBC junior welter-weight Billy Costello in August 1985 the virtually un-known "Lightning" Lonnie Smith told an interviewer for *The Ring* that his model for boxing was that of a chess game: boxing is a "game of control, and, as in chess, this control can radiate in circles *from* the center, or in circles *toward* the center . . . The entire action of a fight goes in a circle; it can be little circles in the middle of the ring or big circles along the ropes, but always a circle. The man who wins is the man who controls the action of the circle." Smith's ring style against Costello was so brazenly idio-syncratic—reminiscent at moments of both Muhammad Ali and Jersey Joe Walcott—that the hitherto undefeated Costello, known as a hard puncher, was totally demoral-ized, outclassed, outboxed. (As he was outfought some months later by a furious Alexis Arguello, who "retired" Costello from the ring.)

Cassius Clay / Muhammad Ali, that most controver-sial of champions, was primarily a brilliant ring strategist, a prodigy in his youth whose fast hands and feet made him virtually impossible for opponents to hit. What joy in the young Ali: in the inimitable arrogance of a heavy-weight who danced about his puzzled opponents with his gloves at waist level, inviting them to hit him—to try it. (What joy, at any rate, in the Ali of films and tapes, even if in somber juxtaposition to the Ali of the present time, overweight, even puffy, his speech and reactions slowed by Parkinson's disease.) It was the young boxer's style when confronted with a "deadly" puncher like Sonny Liston to simply out-think and -maneuver him: never before, and never since, has a heavyweight performed in the ring with such style—an inimitable combination of intelligence, wit, grace, irreverence, cunning. So dazzlingly talented was Ali in his youth that it wasn't clear whether in fact he had what boxers call "heart"—the ability to keep fighting when one has been hurt. In later years, when Ali's speed was diminished, a new and more complex, one might say a greater, boxer emerged, as in the trilogy of fights with Joe Frazier, the first of which Ali lost.

Sugar Ray Leonard, the most charismatic of post-Ali boxers, cultivated a ring style that was a quicksilver balance of opposites, with an overlay of street-wise, playful arrogance (reminiscent, indeed, of Ali), and, for all Leonard's talent, it was only in his most arduous matches (with Hearns and Durán) that it became clear how intelligently ferocious a boxer he really was. Losing once to Durán, he could not lose a second time: his pride would not allow it. Just as pride would not allow Leonard to continue boxing when he suspected he had passed his peak. (Though at the time of this writing Leonard has publicly declared that he wants to return for one major match: *he* is the only man who knows how to beat Marvin Hagler. A matter of ego, Leonard says, as if we needed to be told.)

The self in society, the self in the ring. But there are many selves and there are of course many boxers—ranging from the shy, introverted, painfully inarticulate Johnny Owen (the Welsh bantamweight who died after a bout with Lupe Pintor in 1979) to the frequently manic Muhammad Ali in his prime (Ali whom Norman Mailer compared to a six-foot parrot who keeps screaming at you that he is the center of the stage: "Come here and get me, fool. You can't, 'cause you don't know who I am"); from the legendary bluster of John L. Sullivan to the relative modesty of Rocky Marciano and Floyd Patterson. (Patterson, the youngest man to win the heavyweight title, is said to have been a non-violent person who once helped an opponent pick up his mouthpiece from the canvas. "I don't like to see blood," Patterson explained. "It's different when I bleed, that doesn't bother me because I can't see it." He was no match physically or otherwise for the next heavyweight champion, Sonny Liston.) For every boxer with the reputation of a Roberto Durán there are surely a dozen who are simply "nice guys"—Ray Mancini, Milton McCory, Mark Breland, Gene Hatcher, among many others. Before he lost decisive matches and began the downward trajectory of his career the young Chicago middleweight John Collins was frequently promoted as a veritable split personality, a "Dr. Jekyll / Mr. Hyde" of the ring: the essential (and surely disingenuous) question being, How can a nice courteous young man like you turn so vicious in the ring? Collins's answer was straightforward enough: "When I'm in the ring I'm fighting for my life."

It might be theorized that fighting activates in certain people not only an adrenaline rush of exquisite pleasure but an atavistic self that, coupled with an instinctive sort of tissue-intelligence, a neurological swiftness unknown to "average" men and women, makes for the born fighter, the potentially great champion, the *unmistakably* gifted boxer. An outlaw or non-law self, given the showy accolade "killer instinct." (Though to speak of instinct is always to speak vaguely: for how can "instinct" be isolated from the confluence of factors—health, economic class, familial relations, sheer good or bad luck—that determine a life?) You know the boxer with the killer instinct when the crowd jumps to its feet in a ground swell of delirium in response to his assault against his opponent, no matter if the opponent is the favorite, a "nice guy" no one really wants to see seriously injured.

There is an instinct in our species to fight but is there an instinct to *kill?* And would a "born" killer have the discipline, let alone the moral integrity, to subordinate himself to boxing's rigors in order to exercise it? Surely there are easier ways: we read about them in the daily newspaper. That the fighter, like the crowd he embodies, responds excitedly to the sight of blood—"first blood" being a term from the days of the English Prize Ring— goes without saying; but there are often fight fans shouting for a match to be stopped at the very zenith of the action. My sense of the boxing crowd in a large arena like Madison Square Garden is that it resembles a massive wave containing counter-waves, counter-currents, isolated but bold voices that resist the greater motion toward ecstatic violence. These dissenters are severely critical of referees who allow fights to go on too long.

(I seem to recall my father urging a fight to be stopped: "It's over! It's over! What's the point!" Was it Marciano battering an opponent into submission, or Carmen Basilio? Kid Gavilan? A long time ago, and in our home, the bloody match broadcast over television, hence sanitized. One cannot really imagine the impact of blows on another man's head and body by way of the television screen in its eerily flattened dimensions . . .)

Granted these points, it is nonetheless true that the boxer who functions as a conduit through which the inchoate aggressions of the crowd are consummated will be a very popular boxer indeed. Not the conscientious "boxing" matches but the cheek-by-jowl brawls are likely to be warmly recalled in boxing legend: Dempsey-Firpo, Louis-Schmeling II, Zale-Graziano, Robinson-LaMotta, Pep-Saddler, Marciano-Charles, Ali-Frazier, most recently Hagler-Hearns. Sonny Liston occupies a position *sui generis* for the very truculence of his boxing persona—the air of unsmiling menace he presented to the Negro no less than the white world. (Liston was arrested nineteen times and served two prison terms, the second term for armed robbery.) It may be that former champion Larry Holmes saw himself in this role, the black man's black man empowered by sheer bitterness to give hurt where hurt is due. And, for a while, the Rastafarian Livingstone Bramble, whose vendetta with Ray Mancini seems to have sprung from an unmotivated ill will.

The only self-confessed murderer of boxing distinction seems to have been the welterweight champion Don Jordan (1958–60) who claimed to have been a hired assassin as a boy in his native Dominican Republic. "What's wrong with killing a human?" Jordan asked rhetorically in an interview. "The first time you kill someone, you throw up, you get sick as a dog . . . The second time, no feeling." According to his testimony Jordan killed or helped to kill more than thirty men in the Dominican Republic, without being caught. (He seems in fact to have been in the hire of the government.) After Jordan and his family moved to California he killed a man for "personal" reasons, for which crime he was sent to reform school, aged fourteen: "I burned a man like an animal . . . I staked him to the ground. I wired his hands and his arms, and I put paper around him and I burnt him like an animal. They said, 'You are mentally sick.' " In reform school Jordan was taught how to box: entered the Golden Gloves tournament and won all his matches, and eventually competed in the Olympics, where he did less well. Under the aegis of the Cosa Nostra he turned professional and his career, though meteoric, was short-lived.

In Jake LaMotta's autobiography *Raging Bull* LaMotta attributes his success as a boxer—he was middle-

weight champion briefly, 1949–51, but a popular fighter for many years—to the fact that he didn't care whether he was killed in the ring. For eleven years he mistakenly believed he had murdered a man in a robbery, and, unconfessed, yet guilty, wanting to be punished, LaMotta threw himself into boxing as much to be hurt as to hurt. His background parallels Rocky Graziano's—they were friends, as boys, in reform school—but his desperation was rather more intense than Graziano's (whose autobiography is entitled *Somebody Up There Likes Me:* a most optimistic assumption). LaMotta said in an interview: "I would fight anybody. I didn't care who they were. I even wanted to fight Joe Louis. I just didn't care . . . But that made me win. It gave me an aggression my opponents never saw before. They would hit me. I didn't care if I got hit." When LaMotta eventually learned that his victim had not died, however, his zest for boxing waned, and his career began its abrupt decline. By way of LaMotta's confession and the film based fragmentarily on it, *Raging Bull,* LaMotta has entered boxing folklore: he is the flashy gutter fighter whose integrity will allow him to throw only one fight (in an era in which fights were routinely thrown), done with such ironic disdain that the boxing commission suspends his license.

Traditionally, boxing is credited with changing the lives of ghetto-born or otherwise impoverished youths. It is impossible to gauge how many boxers have in fact risen from such beginnings but one might guess it to be about 99 percent—even at the present time. (Muhammad Ali is said to have been an exception in that his background was not one of desperate poverty: which helps to account, perhaps, for Ali's early boundless confidence.) Where tennis lessons were offered in some youth centers in the Detroit area, many years ago, boxing lessons were offered in Joe Louis's and Ray Robinson's neighborhood—of course. To what purpose would poor black boys learn tennis? LaMotta, Graziano, Patterson, Liston, Hector Camacho, Mike Tyson—all learned to box in captivity, so to speak. (Liston, a more advanced criminal than the others, began taking boxing lessons while serving his second term for armed robbery in the Missouri State Penitentiary.) Boxing is the moral equivalent of war of which, in a radically different context, William James spoke, and it has the virtue—how American, this virtue!—of making a good deal of money for its practitioners and promoters, not all of whom are white.

Indeed, one of the standard arguments for *not* abolishing boxing is in fact that it provides an outlet for the rage of disenfranchised youths, mainly black or Hispanic, who can make lives for themselves by way of fighting one another instead of fighting society.

The disputable term "killer instinct" was coined in reference to Jack Dempsey in his prime: in his famous early matches with Jess Willard, Georges Carpentier, Luis Firpo ("The Wild Bull of the Pampas"), and other lesser known boxers whom he savagely and conclusively beat. Has there ever been a fighter quite like the young Dempsey?—the very embodiment, it seems, of hunger, rage, the will to do hurt; the spirit of the Western frontier come East to win his fortune. The crudest of nightmare figures, Dempsey is gradually refined into an American myth of comforting dimensions. The killer in the ring becomes the New York *restaurateur,* a business success, "the gentlest of men."

Dempsey was the ninth of eleven children born to an impoverished Mormon sharecropper and itinerant railroad worker in Colorado who soon left home, bummed his way around the mining camps and small towns of the West, began fighting for money when he was hardly more than a boy. It was said in awe of Dempsey that his very sparring partners were in danger of being seriously injured— Dempsey didn't like to share the ring with anyone. If he remains the most spectacular (and most loved) champion in history it is partly because he fought when boxing rules were rather casual by our standards; when, for instance, a boxer was allowed to strike an opponent as he struggled to his feet—as in the bizarre Willard bout, and the yet more bizarre bout with Luis Firpo, set beside which present-day heavyweight matches like those of Holmes and Spinks are minuets. Where aggression has to be cultivated in some champion boxers (Tunney, for example) Dempsey's aggression was direct and natural: in the ring, he seems to have wanted to kill his opponent. The swiftness of his attack, his disdain for strategies of defense, endeared him to greatly aroused crowds who had never seen anything quite like him before.

(Dempsey's first title fight, in 1919, against the aging champion Jess Willard, was called at the time "pugilistic murder" and would certainly be stopped in the first round —in the first thirty seconds of the first round—today. Badly out of condition, heavier than the twenty-four-year-old Dempsey by seventy pounds, the thirty-seven-year-old Willard put up virtually no defense against the challenger. Though films of the match show an astonishing resilient, if not foolhardy, Willard picking himself up off the canvas repeatedly as Dempsey knocks him down, by the end of the fight Willard's jaw was broken, his cheekbone split, nose smashed, six teeth broken off at the gum, an eye was battered shut, much damage done to his lower body. Both boxers were covered in Willard's blood. Years later Dempsey's estranged manager Kearns confessed, perhaps fraudulently, that he had "loaded" Dempsey's gloves—treated his hand tape with a talcum substance that turned hard as concrete when wet.)

It was Dempsey's ring style—swift, pitiless, always direct and percussive—that changed American boxing forever. Even Jack Johnson appears stately by contrast.

So far as "killer instinct" is concerned Joe Louis was an anomaly, which no biography of his life—even the most recent, the meticulously researched *Champion—Joe Louis, Black Hero in White America* by Chris Mead—has ever quite explained. If, indeed, one can explain any of our motives, except in the most sweeping psychological and sociological terms. Louis was a modest and self-effacing man outside the ring, but, in the ring, a machine of sorts for hitting—so (apparently) emotionless that even sparring partners were spooked by him. "It's the eyes," one said. "They're blank and staring, always watching you. That blank look—that's what gets you down." Unlike his notorious predecessor Jack Johnson and his yet more notorious successor Muhammad Ali, Joe Louis was forced to live his "blackness" in secret, if at all; to be a *black* hero in *white* America at the time of Louis's coming-of-age cannot have been an easy task. Louis's deadpan expression and his killer's eyes were very likely aspects of the man's strategy rather than reliable gauges of his psyche. And his descent into mental imbalance—paranoia, in particular—in his later years was surely a consequence of the pressures he endured, if not an outsized, but poetically valid, response to the very real scrutiny of others focused upon him for decades.

One of the most controversial of boxing legends has to do with the death of Benny "Kid" Paret at the hands of Emile Griffith in a welterweight match in Madison Square Garden in 1962. According to the story Paret provoked Griffith at their weigh-in by calling him *maricón* (faggot), and was in effect killed by Griffith in the ring that night. Recalling the event years later Griffith said he was only following his trainer's instructions—to hit Paret, to hurt Paret, to keep punching Paret until the referee made him stop. By which time, as it turned out, Paret was virtually dead. (He died about ten days later.)

Though there are other boxing experts, present at the

match, who insist that Paret's death was accidental: it "just happened."

At the present time boxing matches are usually monitored by referees and ringside physicians with extreme caution: a recent match between welterweights Don Curry and James Green was stopped by the referee because Green, temporarily disabled, had lowered his gloves and *might have been hit;* a match between heavyweights Mike Weaver and Michael Dokes was stopped within two minutes of the first round, before the luckless Weaver had time to begin. With some exceptions—the Sandoval-Canizales and the Bramble-Crawley title fights come most immediately to mind—referees have been assuming ever greater authority in the ring so that it sometimes seems that the drama of boxing has begun to shift: not will X knock out his opponent, but will the referee stop the fight before he can do so. In the most violent fights the predominant image is that of the referee hovering at the periphery of the action, stepping in to embrace a weakened or defenseless man in a gesture of paternal solicitude. This image carries much emotional power—not so sensational as the killing blow but suggestive, perhaps, that the ethics of the ring have evolved to approximate the ethics of everyday life. It is as if, in mythical terms, brothers whose mysterious animosity has brought them to battle are saved —absolved of their warriors' enmity—by the wisdom of their father and protector. One came away from the eight-minute Hagler-Hearns fight with the vision of the dazed Hearns, on his feet but not fully conscious, saved by referee Richard Steele from what would have been serious injury, if not death—considering the extraordinary ferocity of Hagler's fighting that night, and the personal rage he seems to have brought to it. ("This was war," Hagler said.) The fight ends with Hearns in Steele's embrace: tragedy narrowly averted.

Of course there are many who disdain such developments. It's the *feminization* of the sport, they say.

I was never knocked out. I've been unconscious, but it's always been on my feet.
—*FLOYD PATTERSON,*
former heavyweight champion of the world

No American sport or activity has been so consistently and so passionately under attack as boxing, for "moral" as well as other reasons. And no American sport evokes so ambivalent a response in its defenders: when asked the familiar question "How can you watch . . . ?" the boxing *aficionado* really has no answer. He can talk about boxing only with others like himself.

In December 1984 the American Medical Association passed a resolution calling for the abolition of boxing

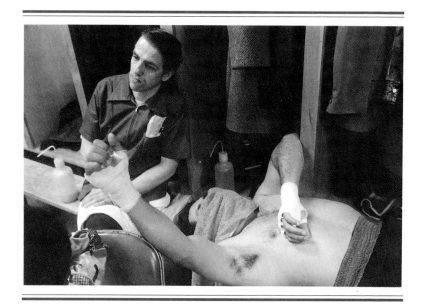

on the principle that while other sports involve as much, or even more, risk to life and health—the most dangerous sports being football, auto racing, hang gliding, mountain climbing, and ice hockey, with boxing in about seventh place—boxing is the only sport in which the objective is to cause injury: the brain is the target, the knockout the goal. In one study it was estimated that 87 percent of boxers suffer some degree of brain damage in their lifetimes, no matter the relative success of their careers. And there is the risk of serious eye injury as well. Equally disturbing, though less plausible, is sociological evidence that media attention focused on boxing has an immediate effect upon the homicide rate of the country. (According to sociologists David P. Phillips and John E. Hensley, the rate rises by an average of 12 percent in the days following a highly publicized fight, for the hypothetical reason that the fight "heavily rewards one person for inflicting violence on another and is at the opposite end of a continuum from a successfully prosecuted murder trial, which heavily punishes one person for inflicting physical violence on another.") Doubtful as these findings are in a culture in which television and movie violence has become routine fare, even for young children, it does seem likely that boxing as a phenomenon *sui generis* stimulates rather than resolves certain emotions. If boxing is akin to classic tragedy in its imitation of action and of life it cannot provide the *katharsis* of pity and terror of which Aristotle spoke.

The variegated history of boxing reform is very

likely as old as boxing itself. As I mentioned earlier, in the days of Pierce Egan's *Boxiana* the Prize Ring was in fact outlawed in England—though the aristocracy, including the Prince Regent, regularly attended matches. Boxing has been intermittently illegal in various parts of the United States and campaigns are frequently launched to ban it altogether. Like abortion it seems to arouse deep and divisive emotions. (Though activists who would outlaw abortion are not necessarily those who would outlaw boxing: puritanical instincts take unpredictable forms.) The relationship between boxing and poverty is acknowledged, but no one suggests that poverty be abolished as the most practical means of abolishing boxing. So frequently do young boxers claim they are in greater danger on the street than in the ring that one has to assume they are not exaggerating for the sake of credulous white reporters.

It is objected too that boxing as a sport is closely bound up with organized crime. Investigations on the federal and state level, over the decades, but most prominently in the fifties, have made the connection unmistakable, though the situation at any time is problematic. One wonders about "suspicious" decisions—are they fixed, or simply the consequence of judges' prejudices? As in Michael Spinks's second, highly controversial win over Larry Holmes, for instance; and the Wilfredo Gomez–Rocky Lockridge match of May 1985 (when judges gave a world junior-lightweight title to a Puerto Rican hometown favorite). And recent televised performances by former

Olympic Gold Medalists and their handpicked opponents have struck the eye of more than one observer as not entirely convincing . . .

Not long ago I saw a film of a long-forgotten fixed fight of Willie Pep's in which Pep allowed himself to be overcome by an underdog opponent: the great featherweight performed as a boxer-turned-actor might be expected to perform, with no excess of zeal or talent. It occurred to me that boxing is so refined, yet so raw a sport that no match can be successfully thrown; the senses simply pick up on what is not happening, what is being held back, as a sort of ironic subtext to what is actually taking place. You can run but you can't hide.

Not boxing in itself but the money surrounding it, the gambling in Las Vegas, Atlantic City, and elsewhere, is the problem, and a problem not likely to be solved. I have made an attempt to read the 135-page single-spaced document "Organized Crime in Boxing: Final Boxing Report of the State of New Jersey Commission of Investigation" of December 1985 and have come to the conclusion that the Commission, which has moved to abolish boxing in New Jersey, was wrongheaded in its initial approach: it should have been investigating organized crime in New Jersey, in which Atlantic City boxing/gambling figures. That the Commission would vote to abolish boxing altogether because of criminal connections suggests a naïveté shading into sheer vindictiveness: one would then be required to abolish funeral parlors, pizzerias, trucking firms, some labor unions. And if gamblers can't gamble on boxing they will simply gamble on football, basketball, baseball—as they already do.

Since boxing has become a multimillion-dollar business under the aegis of a few canny promoters—the most visible being Don King—it is not likely that it will be abolished, in any case. It would simply be driven underground, like abortion; or exiled to Mexico, Cuba, Canada, England, Ireland, Zaire . . . Boxing's history is one of such exigencies, fascinating for what they suggest of the compulsion of some men to fight and of others to be witnesses.

The 1896 heavyweight title match between Ruby Robert Fitzsimmons and Peter Maher, for instance, was outlawed everywhere in the States, so promoters staged it on an isolated sandbar in the Rio Grande River, four hundred miles from El Paso. (Can one imagine?—three hundred men made the arduous journey to witness what was surely one of the most disappointing title bouts in boxing history when Fitzsimmons knocked out Maher in ninety-five seconds.) During Jack Dempsey's prime in the 1920s boxing was outlawed in a number of states, like alcohol, and, like alcohol, seems to have aroused a hysterical public enthusiasm. Dempsey's notorious five minutes with the giant Argentinian Firpo was attended by eighty-five thousand people—most of whom could barely have seen the ring, let alone the boxers; both Dempsey's fights with Gene Tunney were attended by over a hundred thousand people—the first fought in a downpour during which

rain fell in "blinding sheets" for forty minutes on both
boxers and onlookers alike. Photographs of these events
show jammed arenas with boxing rings like postage-sized
altars at their centers, the boxers themselves no more than
tiny, heraldic figures. To attend a Dempsey match was not
to have seen a Dempsey match, but perhaps that was not
the issue.

When Jack Johnson won the heavyweight title in
1908 he had to pursue the white champion Tommy Burns
all the way to Australia to confront him. The "danger" of
boxing at that time—and one of the reasons worried citizens wanted to abolish it—was that it might expose and
humiliate white men in the ring. After Johnson's decisive
victory over the White Hope contender Jim Jeffries there
were in fact race riots and lynchings throughout the
United States; even films of some of Johnson's fights were
outlawed in many states. And because in recent decades
boxing has become a sport in which black and Hispanic
men have excelled it is particularly vulnerable to attack by
white middle-class reformers (the AMA in particular) who
show very little interest in lobbying against equally dangerous Establishment sports like football, auto racing,
thoroughbred horse racing.

The late Nat Fleischer, boxing expert and founder of
The Ring magazine, once estimated that tens of thousands
of injuries have occurred in the ring since the start of
modern boxing in the 1890s—by "modern" meaning the
introduction of the rules of the Marquis of Queensberry
requiring padded gloves, three-minute rounds, one min-

ute's rest between rounds, continuous fighting during rounds. (The bare-knuckle era, despite its popular reputation for brutality, was far less dangerous for fighters—fists break more readily than heads.) Between 1945 and 1985 at least three hundred seventy boxers have died in the United States of injuries directly attributed to boxing. In addition to the infamous Griffith-Paret fight there have been a number of others given wide publicity: Sugar Ray Robinson killed a young boxer named Jimmy Doyle in 1947, for instance, while defending his welterweight title; Sugar Ramos won the featherweight title in 1963 by knocking out the champion Davey Moore, who never regained consciousness; Ray Mancini killed the South Korean Duk Koo-Kim in 1982; former featherweight champion Barry McGuigan killed the Nigerian "Young Ali" in 1983. After the death of Duk Koo-Kim the World Boxing Council shortened title bouts to twelve rounds. (The World Boxing Association retains fifteen. In the era of marathon fights, however—1892 to 1915—men often fought as many as one hundred rounds; the record is one hundred ten, in 1893, over a stupefying seven-hour period. The last scheduled forty-five-round championship fight was between the black title-holder Jack Johnson and his White Hope successor Willard in 1915: the match went twenty-six rounds beneath a blazing sun in Havana, Cuba, before Johnson collapsed.)

To say that the rate of death and injury in the ring is not extraordinary set beside the rates of other sports is to misread the nature of the criticism brought to bear against boxing (and not against other sports). Clearly, boxing's very image is repulsive to many people because it cannot be assimilated into what we wish to know about civilized man. In a technological society possessed of incalculably refined methods of mass destruction (consider how many times over both the United States and the Soviet Union have vaporized each other in fantasy) boxing's display of direct and unmitigated and seemingly natural aggression is too explicit to be tolerated.

Which returns us to the paradox of boxing: its obsessive appeal for many who find in it not only a spectacle involving sensational feats of physical skill but an emotional experience impossible to convey in words; an art form, as I've suggested, with no natural analogue in the arts. Of course it is primitive, too, as birth, death, and erotic love might be said to be primitive, and forces our reluctant acknowledgment that the most profound experiences of our lives are physical events—though we believe ourselves to be, and surely are, essentially spiritual beings.

I ain't never liked violence.
—*SUGAR RAY ROBINSON,*
former welterweight and
middleweight champion of the world

To the untrained eye most boxing matches appear not merely savage but mad. As the eye becomes trained, however, the spectator begins to see the complex patterns that underlie the "madness"; what seems to be merely confusing action is understood to be coherent and intelligent, frequently inspired. Even the spectator who dislikes violence in principle can come to admire highly skillful boxing—to admire it beyond all "sane" proportions. A brilliant boxing match, quicksilver in its motions, transpiring far more rapidly than the mind can absorb, can have the power that Emily Dickinson attributed to great poetry: you know it's great when it takes the top of your head off. (The physical imagery Dickinson employs is peculiarly apt in this context.)

This early impression—that boxing is "mad," or mimics the actions of madness—seems to me no less valid, however, for being, by degrees, substantially modi-

fied. It is never erased, never entirely forgotten or overcome; it simply sinks beneath the threshold of consciousness, as the most terrifying and heartrending of our lives' experiences sink beneath the level of consciousness by way of familiarity or deliberate suppression. So one knows, but does not (consciously) know, certain intransigent facts about the human condition. One does not (consciously) know, but one *knows*. All boxing fans, however accustomed to the sport, however many decades have been invested in their obsession, know that boxing is sheerly madness, for all its occasional beauty. That knowledge is our common bond and sometimes—dare it be uttered?—our common shame.

To watch boxing closely, and seriously, is to risk moments of what might be called animal panic—a sense not only that something very ugly is happening but that, by watching it, one is an accomplice. This awareness, or revelation, or weakness, or hairline split in one's cuticle of a self can come at any instant, unanticipated and unbidden; though of course it tends to sweep over the viewer when he is watching a really violent match. I feel it as vertigo—breathlessness—a repugnance beyond language: a sheerly physical loathing. That it is also, or even primarily, self-loathing goes without saying.

For boxing really isn't metaphor, it is the thing in itself. And my predilection for watching matches on tape, when the outcomes are known, doesn't alter the fact that, as the matches occurred, they occurred in the present tense, and for one time only. The rest is subterfuge—the intellectual's uneasy "control" of his material.

Impossible to see the old, early fights of Dempsey's and not to feel this *frisson* of dread, despite the poor quality of the films, the somewhat antic rhythms of the human figures. Or, I would guess, the trilogy of Zale-Graziano fights about which people speak in awe forty years later. For one man of my acquaintance it was a fight of Joe Louis's, against a long-forgotten opponent. For another, one of the "great" dirty matches of Willie Pep and Sandy Saddler—"little white perfection / and death in red plaid trunks" as the poet Philip Levine has written of that infamous duo. There was Duk Koo-Kim, there was Johnny Owen, in an earlier decade luckless Benny Paret, trapped in the ropes as referee Ruby Goldstein stood frozen, unable to interfere—

And Paret? Paret died on his feet. As he took those eighteen punches something happened to everyone who was in psychic range of the event. Some part of his death reached out to us. One felt it hover in the air. He was still standing in the ropes, trapped as he had been before, he gave some little half-smile of regret, as if he were saying, "I didn't know I was going to die just yet," and then, his head leaning back but still erect, his death came to breathe about him. He began to pass away. He went down more slowly than any fighter had ever gone down, he went down like a large ship which turns on end and slides second by second into its grave.

*As he went down, the sound of Griffith's punches echoed
in the mind like a heavy ax in the distance chopping
into a wet log.*
(NORMAN MAILER, *"Ten Thousand Words a Minute"*)

For one friend of mine it was a bloody fight fought by the
lightweight contender Bobby Chacon that filled him with
horror—though, ironically, Chacon came back to win the
match (as Chacon was once apt to do). For another friend,
a fellow novelist, enamored of boxing since boyhood, it
was the Hagler-Hearns fight of 1985—he was frightened
by his own ecstatic participation in it.

At such times one thinks: What is happening? why
are we here? what does this mean? can't this be stopped?
My terror at seeing Floyd Patterson battered into insensibility by Sonny Liston was not assuaged by my rational
understanding that the event had taken place long ago
and that, in fact, Patterson is in fine health at the present
time, training an adopted son to box. (Liston of course has
been dead for years—he died of a heroin overdose, aged
thirty-eight, in "suspicious" circumstances.) More justified, perhaps, was my sickened sense that boxing is, simply, wrong, a mistake, an outlaw activity for some reason
under the protectorate of the law, when, a few weeks ago
in March 1986, I sat in the midst of a suddenly very quiet
closed-circuit television audience in a suburban Trenton
hall watching bantamweight Richie Sandoval as he lay flat
and unmoving on his back . . . very likely dead of a
savage beating the referee had not, for some reason,

stopped in time. My conviction was that anything was preferable to boxing, anything was preferable to seeing another minute of it, for instance standing outside in the parking lot for the remainder of the evening and staring at the stained asphalt . . .

A friend who is a sportswriter was horrified by the same fight. In a letter he spoke of his intermittent disgust for the sport he has been watching most of his life, and writing about for years: "It's all a bit like bad love— putting up with the pain, waiting for the sequel to the last good moment. And like bad love, there comes the point of being worn out, when the reward of the good moment doesn't seem worth all the trouble . . ."

Yet we don't give up on boxing, it isn't that easy. Perhaps it's like tasting blood. Or, more discreetly put, love commingled with hate is more powerful than love. Or hate.

The spectacle of human beings fighting each other for whatever reason, including, at certain well-publicized times, staggering sums of money, is enormously disturbing because it violates a taboo of our civilization. Many men and women, however they steel themselves, cannot watch a boxing match because they cannot allow themselves to see what it is they are seeing. One thinks helplessly, This can't be happening, even as, and usually quite routinely, it *is* happening. In this way boxing as a public spectacle is akin to pornography: in each case the spectator is made a voyeur, distanced, yet presumably intimately involved, in an event that is not supposed to be happening as it is happening. The pornographic "drama," though as fraudulent as professional wrestling, makes a claim for being about something absolutely serious, if not humanly profound: it is not so much about itself as about the violation of a taboo. That the taboo is spiritual rather than physical, or sexual—that our most valuable human experience, love, is being desecrated, parodied, mocked— is surely at the core of our culture's fascination with pornography. In another culture, undefined by spiritual-emotional values, pornography could not exist, for who would pay to see it?

The obvious difference between boxing and pornography is that boxing, unlike pornography, is not theatrical. It is not, except in instances so rare as to be irrelevant, rehearsed or simulated. Its violation of the taboo against violence ("Thou shalt not kill" in its primordial form) is open, explicit, ritualized, and, as I've said, *routine* —which gives boxing its uncanny air. Unlike pornography (and professional wrestling) it is altogether real: the blood shed, the damage suffered, the pain (usually suppressed or sublimated) are unfeigned. Not for hemophobics, boxing is a sport in which blood becomes quickly irrelevant. The experienced viewer understands that a boxer's bleeding face is probably the least of his worries, and may, in fact, mean nothing at all—one thinks of Rocky Marciano's garishly bloodied but always triumphant face, Marvin Hagler's forehead streaming blood even as he outfought Thomas Hearns. The severely bleeding boxer and his seconds are anxious not about his cut face but about the possibility of the fight being stopped, which means a TKO victory for the opponent. Recall Ray "Boom Boom" Mancini in his second match with Livingstone Bramble, in which he desperately tried to wipe away with his gloves blood pouring from inch-long cuts in his eyelids: twenty-seven stitches were needed to sew up the cuts afterward. (Bramble, pragmatic like all boxers, naturally worked Mancini's damaged eyes as frequently as he could. Of 674 blows struck by Bramble 255 struck him in the face.)

Just as the boxer is trained to fight until he can't go on, so he is trained, or is by nature equipped, to fight unconscious on his feet. The image is indelibly imprinted in my memory of the doomed South Korean lightweight Duk Koo-Kim struggling to rise from the canvas after a blow of Mancini's burst a blood vessel in his brain—as if his body possessed its own demonic will even at the threshold of death. It is said that Joe Louis, badly stunned by Max Schmeling in their first fight, fought unconscious for several rounds—his beautifully conditioned body performing its trained motions like clockwork. (And it was during this losing bout that Louis's prodigious talent for endurance, and therefore for great boxing, manifested itself.) So customary is this sort of "fearless" boxing that the behavior of heavyweight Jesse Ferguson in his February 1986 match with Mike Tyson—clinching, holding on to Tyson's gloves, refusing in effect to fight—struck the eye as unnatural when of course it was utterly natural, the way the average man would behave in so desperate a situation. But boxing is contrary to nature.

One of the paradoxes of boxing is that the viewer inhabits a consciousness so very different from that of the boxer as to suggest a counter-world. "Free" will, "sanity," "rationality"—our characteristic modes of consciousness —are irrelevant, if not detrimental, to boxing in its most extraordinary moments. Even as he disrobes himself ceremonially in the ring the great boxer must disrobe himself of both reason and instinct's caution as he prepares to fight.

Dustin Hoffman recalls a boxing match he had seen as a boy: as the triumphant boxer left the ring to pass up the aisle, an ecstatic fight fan, male, followed closely after him, wiping all he could of the sweat from the boxer's body onto himself.

An observer is struck by boxing's intense preoccupation with its own history; its continuous homage to a gallery of heroes—or are they saints? At Muhammad Ali's Deer Lake, Pennsylvania, training camp the names of heavyweight champions—Louis, Marciano, Liston, Patterson, et al.—were painted in white letters on massive iconographic boulders. "Jack Dempsey" named himself for the middleweight champion Jack Dempsey (1884–91 —known as Dempsey "The Nonpareil" because he outboxed every man he fought). "Sugar Ray" Leonard named himself boldly after "Sugar Ray" Robinson—an act of audacity that did not prove embarrassing. If Marvin Hagler shaves his head, the image of Rubin "Hurricane" Carter comes to mind, and, beyond him, that of Jack Johnson himself—the first and very likely the greatest of defiantly *black* boxers, whom Cassius Clay / Muhammad Ali admired as well. So frequently are a few names evoked— Dempsey, Louis, Marciano, Pep, Robinson—one might think these boxers were our contemporaries and not champions of eras long past.

If boxing exhausts most of its practitioners in a Darwinian struggle for survival like virtually no other, it so honors a very few, so enshrines them in the glamour of immortality, surely the danger is justified? As in any religion, present and past are magically one; Time, even death, are defeated. The dead immortals are always with us, not only their names and the hazy outlines of careers recalled, but individual bouts, moments when decisive punches were thrown and caught, the size of a boxer's fist, the measurement of his reach, his age when he began and when he retired, his record of wins, losses, draws. The uppercut Jack Johnson used against Stanley Ketchel in 1909—the famous Fitzsimmons "shift" of 1897 (when

Fitzsimmons defeated Gentleman Jim Corbett for the heavyweight title)—the wicked left hook with which Jack Dempsey caught a distracted Jack Sharkey in 1927—Rocky Marciano's several right-hand knockout punches—Cassius Clay's mystery punch in the first minute of the first round of his second match with Sonny Liston—the left hook of Joe Frazier that knocked Muhammad Ali on his back in the fifteenth round of their first fight: all are commemorated. The typical boxing writer's imagination is not so much stimulated by his subject as enflamed. Dream matches are routinely fantasized in which boxers of different eras meet one another—Marciano-Dempsey, Louis-Ali, Hagler-Robinson, the 1961 Sonny Liston and the 1973 George Foreman. Boxers of different weights are thrown together—how would Willie Pep or Benny Leonard or Roberto Durán have done against Joe Louis, *equipped with the necessary poundage?* Though preoccupation with past records is common to most sports there is something unusually intense about it in boxing, perhaps because, in boxing, the individual is so very alone, or seems so. Like the saint he gives the impression of having arrived at his redemption by unflagging solitary effort.

The boxing past exists in an uncannily real and vital relationship with the present. The dead are not dead, or not merely dead. When, for instance, Larry Holmes made his ill-advised attempt to equal Rocky Marciano's record (forty-nine wins, no losses) it seemed suddenly that Marciano was living again, his name and photograph in all the papers, interviews with his family published. Michael

Spinks resurrected not only Billy Conn, the light-heavy-weight champion who was defeated in a famous match by Joe Louis in 1941 (and again in 1946) but any number of other light-heavyweight champions who were defeated by heavyweight champions—Georges Carpentier, Tommy Loughran, Joey Maxim, the indefatigable Archie Moore. The spectacular first round of the Hagler-Hearns match provoked reminiscences of "the greatest first rounds of all time." (Number one remains Dempsey-Firpo, 1923.) *The Ring*'s Hall of Fame—to which controversial Jake La-Motta was only recently elected—corresponds to the pantheon of saints elected by the Vatican except it is in fact more finely calibrated, its saints arranged under various groupings and subgroupings, and its balloting highly complex. (Indeed, no intellectual journal in the States is more scrupulously attentive to its history than this famous boxing magazine, founded by Nat Fleischer in 1922, in which past, present, and a hypothesized future are tirelessly examined, and in which one finds articles on such subjects as "The Greatest Disappointments in Ring History," "The Greatest Mismatches," "The Greatest Left Hooks," "When a Good Little Man *Did* Defeat a Good Big Man.")

It is as if by way of the most strenuous exigencies of the physical self a boxer can—sometimes—transcend the merely physical; he can, if he is lucky, be absolved of his mortality. The instinct is of course closely allied with the desire for fame and riches (those legendary champions with their purple Cadillacs!) but is not finally identical with it. If the boxing ring is an altar it is not an altar of sacrifice solely but one of consecration and redemption. Sometimes.

". . . I am a sophomore at [an upstate New York SUNY campus] and when I'm at school I work out at a downtown gym 5 days a week. The gym is completely removed from the atmosphere of school in every way. Through boxing I manage to release aggression . . . I've yet to have my first amateur fight. My trainer says when I'm sparring I don't look like I want to hurt my man. 'You gotta want to hurt him, because he's sure going to hurt you.' I'm afraid my lack of bloodlust stems from a fear of going too far, physically and/or mentally. However far I push myself in the gym something in me is holding back . . .

"I have very little idea what it was that attracted me to boxing in the first place. No one in my immediate experience ever had the least interest in it. What started as a little fooling around at the Y soon turned into almost an obsession . . . Over Christmas break I had a bad experience I'd rather not repeat. The trainer gave me a break, said he'd let me train with the team for a while, and I wound up sparring the first night with a fellow who outmatched me pretty badly in experience. I took a 3-round beating, never letting him knock me down, but

taking plenty of punishment, mostly jabs that landed on or around my nose, which I was sure must be broken by the end of the second round. After practice the trainer told me I had a hell of a lot of heart. Don't blow your nose, he said, or your eyes will black, and be here tomorrow. Driving home I knew 'heart' meant crazy or stupid or both, but still the wave of elation I felt matched the fear and trepidation that came over me before I entered that ring . . . and afterwards anticipating facing my parents. I didn't leave the house for days after that, I became depressed and embarrassed, I thought that perhaps boxing wasn't worth it after all, maybe I couldn't cut it, and I was afraid I'd already lost whatever looks I had. My face swelled up to an unspeakably ugly apparition, and I carried two black eyes for months afterwards.

"I took an introductory course to poetry last semester and through it I became convinced that the best way to convey my reasons for and feelings about boxing would be through poetry . . ."

—excerpts of letters to
the author from a young boxer

If they cut my bald head open,
they will find one big boxing glove.
That's all I am. I live it.
—MARVIN HAGLER

T hough boxing has long been popular in many countries and under many forms of government, dictatorships no less than democracies, surely its popularity in the States since the days of John L. Sullivan has a good deal to do with what Americans honor as the spirit of the individual—his "physical" spirit—in defiance of the State. The remarkable rise of boxing in the 1920s in particular can be seen as a consequence of the diminution of the individual vis-à-vis society; the gradual attrition of personal freedom, will, and strength—"masculine," to be sure, but not solely masculine. What more appropriate hero for the times than the pitiless ex-barroom brawler Jack Dempsey of Manassa, Colorado? Today, the "totalitarian" consciousness in the Eastern bloc of nations is clearly a function of the state while in the Western bloc it has come to seem a function of technology, if not history —inexorable fate. How to master these ever more difficult machines, how even to learn their language, when so many of us are illiterate . . . The individual exists in his physical supremacy, but does the individual matter?

In the magical space of the boxing ring so disturbing a question has no claim. There as in no other public arena does the individual as a unique physical being assert himself; there, for a dramatic if fleeting period of time, the great world with its moral and political complexities, its terrifying impersonality, ceases to exist. Men fighting one another with only their fists and their cunning are all contemporaries, all brothers, belonging to no historical

time. The crowd, borne along with them, belongs to no historical time. "He can run but he can't hide"—so said Joe Louis before his great fight with Conn in 1941. In the brightly lit ring, man is *in extremis,* performing an atavistic rite or *agon* for the mysterious solace of those who can participate only vicariously in such drama: the drama of life in the flesh. Boxing has become America's tragic theater.

ACKNOWLEDGMENTS

Heller, Peter. *In This Corner: Forty World Champions Tell Their Stories* (Simon & Schuster, New York, 1973).

McCallum, John D. *The World Heavyweight Boxing Championship: A History* (Chilton Book Co., Radnor, Pennsylvania, 1974).

McIlvanney, Hugh. *McIlvanney on Boxing: An Anthology* (Beaufort Books, New York, 1983).

Mead, Chris. *Champion: Joe Louis; Black Hero in White America* (Charles Scribner's Sons, New York, 1985).

Odd, Gilbert. *Encyclopedia of Boxing* (Crescent Books, New York, 1983).

The Ring magazine (New York, New York).

Schulian, John. *Writers' Fighters and Other Sweet Scientists* (Andrews & McMeel, Fairway, Kansas, 1983).

Background material for the section on "opponents" was drawn from articles by Michael Shapiro and Budd Schulberg appearing in the New York *Times* and *Newsday* respectively.

Sociologists David P. Phillips and John E. Hensley in "When Violence Is Rewarded or Punished: The Impact